Paula Easley's
WAREHOUSE FOOD
COOKBOOK

Merril Press
Bellevue, Washington

First Edition
Published by Merril Press
Box 1682
Bellevue, Washington 98005
Telephone 425-454-9470

Text and design by Classic Design and Typography. Cover by LaFleur Printing & Design.
Copy editing by Richard Vollertsen and Annette Hinman-Patterson.
Typeset in Goudy Oldstyle.

LIBRARY OF CONGRESS CATALOGING-IN-PUBLICATION DATA

Easley, Paula (Paula Pence)
   [Warehouse food cookbook]
   Paula Easley's warehouse food cookbook. – 1st ed.
      p. cm.
   ISBN 0-936783-24-9
   1. Quantity cookery. 2. Low budget cookery. 3. Customer clubs.
I. Title. II. Title: Warehouse food cookbook.
TX820.E28 1999
641.5'7–dc21
                                                    99-24389
                                                          CIP

PRINTED IN THE UNITED STATES OF AMERICA

— C O N T E N T S —

ACKNOWLEDGEMENTS

The author acknowledges the thoughtful and creative contributions
of the following:

*Cherise Acosta, Teri Arnold, Linda Brown, Diane Carpenter, Peter Combs,
Chris Hitchcock, Cathy Janvrin, Barbara Kirbach, Stephanie LaFleur,
Leila Lee, Charles Leggett, Suzanne Linford,
Carole McGillis, Esther Morelli, Elizabeth Nuzum, Bill O'Keeffe,
Ginger Combs-Ramirez, Dolores Ritchie, Von Roberts, Don Shain,
Sally Suddock, Doug and Joanie Thompson, Don Wilcox.
And, special thanks to my relentless editors,
Rick Vollertsen and Annette Hinman-Patterson.*

DEDICATION

This book is dedicated to my daughters, Kathryn and Laura Easley. Kathryn
inherited the family's rampant cooking genes and is a superb cook. Laura nagged
me unmercifully to write the book, then helped me through the process of
bringing it to completion by always being there.

— ABOUT THE AUTHOR—

Paula Easley began cooking when she was tall enough to reach the stove burners. As the designated cook for five siblings, her earliest influence was southern cooking, the only style "allowed" in her hometown of Louisville, Kentucky. Still strongly partial to it, her other favorites are Mexican, Italian, Spanish, Southwestern and Island cookery.

Since 1962, the author has lived and cooked in rural and urban Alaska where she learned to make do with whatever was available and affordable. The Academy of Culinary Arts, Le Cordon Bleu, and the Culinary Institute of America were educational options she declined in favor of the Chef's School of Hard Knocks, where she earned her degree. Easley believes anyone, with a little imagination, planning and common sense, can routinely prepare outstanding meals, no matter how pressed for time or money.

Despite a busy career as an association executive, federal lobbyist and economic development professional, the author continues to enjoy home cooking and entertaining, making it appear fun and effortless. This book responds to the urging of family and friends to explain how she does it.

When her schedule permits, Easley travels to Alamos, Sonora, Mexico, where her sister Diane Carpenter, an Alaska restaurant and hotel proprietor, owns a lovely colonial home. Some of the author's recipes reflect the Sonoran influence. It was in Alamos that many of the book's recipes were tested. All who participated in the testing are alive and in good health.

INTRODUCTION

I like to eat well, and I love good home cooking. (Who doesn't?) My problem – besides having "champagne tastes and a beer pocketbook" – always has been finding the time to prepare my family's favorite foods. Shopping and cooking a meal from scratch after work was exhausting. Dining out took too much time and was far too expensive for the family budget. I also liked to cook for friends in a relaxed atmosphere, but procrastination prevailed. A solution was clearly needed if I were to have it all.

My solution was "warehouse shopping" and "ingredient cooking," which I will explain later. In the meantime, I'll share my five good reasons to shop for food at the membership warehouses (Sam's Club and Costco in my town) and to learn the secrets of ingredient cooking:

(1) To save time,
(2) To save money,
(3) To eat healthier,
(4) To have fun, and
(5) To entertain like a pro.

Once I got the hang of this new approach, I was rewarded with a *minimum* of ten extra hours a week to use as I pleased. In addition, our diets improved substantially, I saved a ton of money, enjoyed meeting the challenge, and felt less frazzled. The secrets in this book will help you do the same.

While the techniques I learned evolved over many years and thousands of meals, a treasured experience was what got me started some 30 years ago. Cooking at our family lodge in bush Alaska (no grocery stores within 300 air miles) presented formidable challenges that may give you some insight.

Groceries for the lodge and trading post arrived just twice a year on the spring and fall barges. This called for innovative (read: desperate) measures. After unloading, hauling and sorting hundreds of cases of dry, canned and frozen foods came the urgent task of doing something with the fresh produce. Carrots, onions, bell peppers, turnips, potatoes, apples, oranges, lemons, cabbage, celery, yams, and squash all had to be dealt with while they still resembled live substances.

With limited freezer space, we had no choice but to get rid of the unusable parts and prepare the fruits and vegetables based on how they would ultimately be used in recipes. That's what we did, and that is one of the secrets of ingredient cooking. The food listings in this book give updated, explicit directions for doing this yourself.

Many of our favorite recipes called for old-fashioned stocks made from meat, seafood and fowl. The very best stews, soups, casseroles, sauces and gravies owe their rich flavor to these essential stocks. Back then, we made meat stocks from moose and caribou bones, seasoned with vegetables and spices, and cooked on a wood stove for days.

This one-time activity provided months of delicious seasoning as the final product, defatted, strained, and frozen into handy 4-ounce cubes, was instantly available. Today I buy the excellent beef and chicken bases on the market and a fine demi-glace from a gourmet mail order house. But I still remember the incomparable aroma of homemade stock simmering on the wood stove.

When I moved to the city, my bush cooking techniques largely fell by the wayside. Meal-planning began while driving home from work. As a young widow and working mother, I found fresh fruits and vegetables to be out of reach on my salary. It bothered me greatly that my children weren't able to eat the kinds of foods I knew they should have. That finally changed when Costco and Sam's Club located in Anchorage. Thanks to these operations, I have since served great homemade meals and party food at far less cost, and the people I serve eat higher – and healthier – on the food chain.

I know there are thousands of single parents, working couples, families of all sizes, and people cooking just for themselves, who can benefit by this sensible, new approach to food preparation. You don't need to be a Julia Child clone to succeed at it. Just remember, cooking is a very forgiving activity. You can substitute any number of ingredients, quantities, procedures or temperatures when necessary, and still end up with food that you will be proud to serve. With my help, I hope you'll give it a try.

PART I:

Cooking

with

Warehouse Food

—INGREDIENT COOKING SECRETS—

"Ingredient cooking" means preparing a specific food in larger quantities than normal for ultimate use in a variety of recipes. Let's say you just bought a flat of gorgeous, almost-vine-ripened "warehouse" tomatoes, twelve large ones. Here's how you might use them for two people:

Bacon, lettuce and tomato sandwiches – 1
Tossed green salad – 1
Fresh salsa with cilantro and green chiles – 2
Gazpacho, a chilled salad-soup – 3
Tomato marinara sauce to be frozen – 4
Spanish rice – 2
Roasted tomato soup to serve with garlic croutons – 4
Okra, corn and tomato casserole to eat or freeze – 3
Stuffed tomatoes with tuna or chicken salad – 2

Oops. We just used 22 tomatoes! If you had some left, you could dice and simmer them with onions, and freeze the mixture for various other dishes. The important thing is to buy them with the idea that you will use them, not let them rot in the vegetable bin.

My strategy is to prepare several ingredients at once. Altogether, it might take 20 minutes to accomplish. I would make the marinara sauce, roast and peel the tomatoes for the soup, and prepare the okra, corn and tomato casserole, all of which freeze beautifully.

With the time-tested techniques in this book, conveniently included with each food item, you will envision foods you buy or have on hand as *ingredients* for any number of popular dishes that can be put together in minutes. You will quickly discover that getting to the fresh-tasting finished product will be unbelievably easy, cheap, and fast.

There's no need to plan a month's menus, buy a carload of groceries, or have cooking, canning and freezing marathons to benefit from ingredient cooking. Most of us live hectic, busy lives and lack the time or motivation to go that far. With this book as a guide, however, you'll develop a flexible style of food preparation that lets you enjoy fresh food at its peak, along with other food items that lend themselves to easy combinations.

If you would like to serve fabulous *Roasted Orange and Yellow Pepper Soup* tonight, no problem; add some chicken broth to your frozen pureed ingredients, and you'll have it. If it's *Pasta with Basil-Pine Nut Pesto*, not a problem; cook the pasta and add your prepared pesto.

Maybe you're in the mood for scrumptious *Walnut Stuffed Whole Mushrooms* followed by *"Fresh"Asparagus Soup* in January – you'll need maybe 20 minutes. Or, how about *Old-fashioned Bread Pudding with Tart Lemon Sauce* for dessert? It will be ready when the main course is removed from the table.

For another example, pick up a 10-pound package of that good-old standby, lean ground beef. Meatloaf sounds good, doesn't it?

With your fresh or frozen supply of chopped celery, onion, bell peppers and mushrooms, and your homemade seasoned breadcrumbs, you have the basics for any number of great meatloaf recipes. We'll use three pounds of ground beef and make two. Put one in the oven for dinner and freeze the other. Now you're getting it. What to do with the rest of the meat? That depends on what you like to eat.

Many ground beef recipes begin with "brown the meat and chopped onions." So, why not do it now, *before* it goes into the freezer. You've saved time doing it all at once, gotten rid of the excess fat, and eliminated one messy food preparation step. Your beef and onion mix will take up less room in the freezer and still leave you options for deciding how to use it. We'll prepare three pounds that way.

When assembling your final recipe – whatever it is, casseroles, chili, meat pies, pasta sauce, pirogi, taco salad, tostados, etc., you are just minutes away from serving time.

You may want a stack of hamburger patties; for that we'll use two pounds. A friend of mine takes the hamburgers a step further. He grills them over charcoal with his famous sauce, freezes them and takes the frozen patty to work. At lunchtime it gets a quick jolt in the microwave.

For the last two pounds you could mix the meat with onions, rice, tomatoes and seasonings for stuffed bell peppers, or, how about some cocktail-sized meatballs? So wonderful with a spicy sauce. Besides, you are much more likely to have friends over when the mood strikes or to volunteer your home for an impromptu meeting if you have some appetizers stashed away.

Let's say you do not want to cook today, period. You will have sautéed and frozen some of the warehouse boneless, skinless chicken breasts or thighs. Thaw a package, pull off some meat, add lettuce, tomato, avocado, cilantro, onion and homemade salsa, then pack it all into a Reser's giant-sized Basil-Pesto flour tortilla. Or, try the tomato-flavored, jalapeño, cheese or spinach tortillas. Ten each of three flavors come in a package from the warehouse. Use what you want and freeze the rest. There are dozens of tasty tortilla fillings that you can quickly prepare and enjoy just as much.

These examples give you an idea where you can go with the ingredient style of cooking. The best way for you to get the picture, though, is to try it yourself. Much more on the "how to" is in the individual food listings.

—GETTING STARTED—

It's human nature to resist change. If I can convince you of the benefits of warehouse food shopping and ingredient cooking, I guarantee you will become a happy convert. First, do this:

❖ List 10 to 20 of your favorite menus or dinner meals, even foods you can't afford. Be extravagant, because they will be affordable with the money you'll save.

❖ On a calendar, spread these favorites over two weeks or a month. Be realistic. Put on your calendar the days you are likely to eat dinner out or order takeout food. This meal-planning exercise will be fun and rewarding.

❖ Translate your meal plans into a shopping list, referring to the listings and recipes in the food section.

❖ Do an inventory of your kitchen to determine if you have the necessary packaging materials, access to freezer space, and a place to store non-freezer items. Review the section on Buying Big. Then go shopping.

—WAREHOUSE SHOPPING—

I first began shopping the warehouse clubs to save money. What kept me returning was the quality. Fresh, firm grapes that stayed perfect more than a week. Packaged romaine lettuce that remained crisp and unblemished for two weeks. Flawless strawberries. Large, crunchy bell peppers. Gourmet cheeses. Fresh pasta and sauces. The finest meat and seafood. Picture-perfect mushrooms. Before I knew it, I was hooked on warehouse shopping.

If you like to save money, you'll find the warehouse stores offer members surprisingly big savings. The advantage they have over typical food suppliers is the cashflow generated by our annual membership fees, giving them incomparable negotiating and buying power. To benefit from these savings, however, we must make some easy changes in the way we shop, store and prepare food.

A significant deterrent to food shopping at the warehouse superstores is the quantity one must often purchase to obtain these savings. Many shoppers, especially singles, choose not to take advantage of quantity food buying for fear the food items will go to waste. There's no need to waste anything, once you learn a few of my tricks.

Quantity buying is not wasteful if you shop with a strategy in mind. If you're adventurous enough to try it, you will save time and money, have fun doing it, and eat fabulous, healthful meals.

In the food section, I will help you make savvy purchases and tell you how to store and maintain the quality of what you buy. Best of all, you will learn successful ways to transform your purchases into ready-to-use ingredients for your favorite dishes. With these secrets you will make efficient use of food in your ingredient arsenal whenever you're in the mood to cook. It will help even more when you're *not* in the mood and want a good home-cooked meal.

Warehouse shopping enables a unique approach to food preparation that lets you do most of the work when you want to fit it into your schedule. It capitalizes on quantity buying opportunities now available in hundreds of communities across the North American Continent, Europe and Asia. These opportunities were made possible by the rapid expansion of membership warehouse operations such as Costco Wholesale, Price Club (now PriceCostco) and Sam's Club, a Wal-Mart division. (See the Appendix for store locations in the United States, Mexico and Canada as of January 1999.)

If you have just joined a warehouse club and are anxious to consider this new way of cooking, I suggest you first browse the fruit and vegetable sections of the book and select two or three items for your initial ingredient cooking experiment. For example, read up on tomatoes, bell peppers and onions, buy and prepare them for storage, then jump right into the recipes. Get that project finished before undertaking another. I want you to have fun doing this!

As more and more membership warehouse clubs are established nearby, the likelihood that you can visit one weekly increases. But first-timers should be prepared. The warehouses and their parking lots are huge, and often crowded. Dress comfortably; the trip can be tiring. (Shoppers with mobility problems should check with the warehouse clubs in their areas, as many have electric carts available.) Before stacking too many food items in your shopping cart, remember you have to unload them at the checkout counter, pack them in your vehicle, unload them at home and find a place to put them.

To make sure you have energy for the "at home" work, do what more and more warehouse shoppers do. They make their weekly trip a social outing, taking friends or family along. Involving children in the project is an excellent way to teach them planning, thrift, nutrition and food preservation techniques.

But "Wait!" you say. "I am just one person. This can't be for *me*!" Yes, it can. I've shopped and cooked for myself for years, and I'm a confirmed warehouse food junkie. My warehouse cooking techniques are for you if you like to cook, if you want to save time and money, and if you do the necessary preparation and packaging.

Are warehouse prices always cheaper? Check them out. As a smart shopper, you'll want to arm yourself with price lists and local grocery ads. Sometimes grocery specials and loss leaders equal or beat the warehouse prices, but make sure the quality is comparable. All the warehouses list unit prices, which makes it easier to do these comparisons.

It also pays to keep a close watch on pricing between the warehouse stores themselves. For instance, Sam's Club reduces prices of items nearing their pull date, as well as perishables not likely to be sold quickly enough at regular prices.

On one trip to Sam's, I cashed in on Tropicana Grovestand fresh orange juice at two 64-ounce cartons for 99 cents! This top-quality product usually sells for more than $3.25 each at the supermarket. I picked up four of the double-packs and froze three (with no noticeable loss in flavor).

Other Suppliers. You do not have to be a member of Costco Wholesale or Sam's Club to practice the techniques outlined in this book. Many of the food items mentioned in this book are available from other reliable sources.

Your community may have food cooperatives that offer substantial price breaks for quantity purchases. Health food stores and farmers' markets are other good sources, as are co-op buying clubs in your area. Check out your local wholesale food distributors. Most have catalogs you can study.

While wholesale distributors seldom advertise to the general public, most are happy to accommodate any customer willing to purchase in case lots. They also are likely to carry a far more extensive inventory than the membership clubs do.

Supermarkets are another potential source. Encouraged by the warehouse competition, many now have bulk quantities available at lower prices. They have also instituted improvements in fruit and vegetable packaging that keep the products fresh longer. It doesn't hurt to ask if they'll offer discounts for buying case lots of virtually any item – you may be surprised with the response.

Shopping for staples. It makes sense to buy only what you can use within a reasonable timeframe – say six months to a year. If your storage room is limited, team with a friend for staples such as rice, dried beans, pasta, flour, sugar, salt, cooking oils, yeast, powdered milk, coffee beans, etc. They are all excellent bargains – rice, for example. A ten-pound bag of top-quality long-grain rice cost me just around $2.50 (October 1998).

Naturally, all these items must be properly stored to preserve their freshness and protect them from food pests. That is why I've gone to great lengths in the section entitled "Buying Big: How to Make it Last" to explain the process. Specific storage recommendations are also included with each food listing.

Share the wealth. You can always donate extra food supplies to needy families or share with neighbors who have difficulty getting around. Recently two friends and I shopped at Costco, making it a pleasant social occasion. When we got home and were dividing up cases of grapefruit, Vidalia onions, mangos and oranges, we decided to cook up some casseroles for our local homeless shelter. One friend stirred up a gallon of white sauce, the other cooked and sliced up a pile of potatoes, and I prepared onions, peppers and some leftover cheeses from my freezer supply. We froze our unbaked scalloped potatoes in foil-lined dishes and transported them to the shelter later, minus the dishes. Everyone benefitted!

By stocking a variety of staples and keeping a good supply of prepared "ingredients" on hand, getting to the finished product is unbelievably easy and convenient, and the food you serve will be nutritious and fresh tasting. As you begin implementing this style of food preparation, you will develop many improvements and specialties that suit your own tastes and fit your lifestyle. I am confident you will enjoy the challenge and the rewards.

—EATING HEALTHIER—

Nutrition experts seldom miss a chance to tell us that "we are what we eat." (I am *not* an avocado.) While I'm sure the phrase wasn't meant to be interpreted literally, research affirms the importance of lifelong healthful eating habits.

A look at mortality statistics attests to this. According to U. S. Government publications, two-thirds of all deaths, including coronary heart disease, atherosclerosis, stroke, diabetes and some 35 percent of all cancer deaths, are diet-related.

Today, more cancer deaths are linked with poor nutrition than to any other cause, including tobacco and alcohol. This may seem surprising, because it is human nature to attribute these deaths to external influences, such as pollution, rather than to influences we control, like what we eat, drink or smoke.

Scientists now say a long-term diet high in fruits, vegetables and fiber reduces lung and colon cancer *risk* by 30-40%, and stomach cancer by 60%. The National Cancer Institute (NCI) itself reports that, in reviews of some 150 epidemiological studies, the diet connection to prevention of lung, colon and stomach cancers is strong.

Several studies associate high vegetable intake with reduced incidences of many other types of cancer, such as cancers of the mouth, pharynx, larynx, esophagus, lung, stomach, colon, rectum, bladder and cervix. So, while we may not be able to find a cure when disease has taken over our cells, the evidence is strong that diet plays a major role in *prevention*.

To "cover the bases," (since no one knows precisely which fruits and vegetables are the most effective disease fighters), the experts advise eating them all. Eat plenty of berries, dark green, yellow and orange fruits, dried fruits, and a broad selection of vegetables. They are primary sources of folate, carotenoids and other antioxidants, fiber, various phytochemicals, and Vitamins A, C, and E.

The 5 A Day Cancer Prevention Program. With recommendations of the 5 A Day Program (five servings of fruits and vegetables every day) publicized by the National Cancer Institute and other private and government organizations, many consumers now recognize the critical role of nutrition in preventing cancer. Five servings are the minimum recommended; more is better. For a free brochure with more specifics, call the Cancer Information Service, 1-800-4-CANCER.

Unfortunately, national surveys reveal that less than 25% of the U.S. population follows the 5 A Day Program. That's a rather discouraging statistic for the Land of Plenty. Perhaps too few Americans realize the importance of good nutrition to overall disease prevention. It is more likely, however, that many of us (especially those with large families) believe such a program is too expensive.

No question about it, the cost of most fresh fruits and vegetables at the supermarket is hefty. When a fresh orange costs a dollar, many of us don't buy oranges. When you can buy a case for half the price, though, you might. Of course every fruit and vegetable doesn't have to be fresh to qualify for the 5 A Day Program. While fresh is the ideal choice, frozen, canned and dried foods are perfectly acceptable, and a "serving" is not all that much.

What's a Serving?
One-half cup of fruit
3/4 cup of 100% juice
1/2 cup cooked vegetable
1 cup fresh leafy vegetable
1/4 cup dried fruit

Unexpected Allies in Disease Prevention.
Unquestionably, the warehouse clubs have made food more affordable. People who regularly shop the warehouses say their diets contain far more top-quality fresh foods than before. By providing consumers less costly food, the membership warehouse clubs have, perhaps unwittingly, assumed a starring role in the fight against cancer and other diet-related diseases.

Because they have made quality food available and more affordable to millions of consumers (Costco alone has more than 27 million members), the warehouse stores deserve commendation by government and private health agencies promoting the disease prevention message. Who knows how many cases of cancer and other diseases can be prevented as more families make good nutrition a priority?

PART II:

Best Foods
for
Ingredient Cooking

MEAT, POULTRY AND SEAFOOD

INTRODUCTION

Just thinking about the marvelous meat selection on display at the warehouse stores makes me hungry for prime rib, marinated pork tenderloin, barbecued ribs, a rack of lamb, or a succulent beef filet. These and other large cuts of meat freeze beautifully and remain stable for up to a year if properly wrapped and quickly frozen.

Large cuts of meat can provide many meals with good planning. A whole pork loin is a frequent purchase for my kitchen.

I partially freeze the loin to make slicing easier; then most of it gets sliced paper thin, pounded with a mallet, and flash frozen. The scallopini are packaged with waxed paper between each one. You can hardly find a quicker dinner entree than pork scallopini.

Over the years home cooks and popular restaurants have made a gradual transition toward using small amounts of meat in combination recipes rather than serving a large piece of meat separately. Restaurant patrons are apparently satisfied with these smaller portions because some of the more popular menu items are stir-fried dishes, filled pasta, veal scallopini, pork medallions, tiny lamb chops, skewered meats, pizza, chili, meat/vegetable filled tortillas, meat/salad combinations, etc. More emphasis is placed on preparation than quantity, and I love tasting the ingenious way chefs season their specialties.

If barbecued beef and pork ribs are on your favorite food list, make serving them easy. When you bring home a large supply, cut and season them the way you like. Put the meat in a large roasting or broiler pan and roast slowly, uncovered, until tender. Doing this before freezing the meat gets rid of the excess fat and the mess. Then, when it's rib time, just add the barbecue sauce and toss them on the grill or in the oven, frozen. For entertaining, this is the only way to go.

Ground beef, pork, veal, sausage, Italian sausage, ham, and sliced pepperoni and salami for pizza are excellent meat products for your ingredient storehouse. Not only are they suitable for many recipes, they can often be used interchangeably. I don't recommend having them on hand, however, unless you have recipes in mind for using them within two months. Otherwise they can suffer flavor deterioration.

Ham and bacon are two items better kept under refrigeration than frozen; they seem to lose their flavor quickly in the freezer, and the ham can become watery. Pieces of each kept for flavoring soups and beans are OK, but that's about all I would recommend, unless they are vacuum-sealed. Then they keep for longer periods. I do like having cooked bacon bits handy for seasoning; a small jar of it has a special place in my kitchen freezer door.

Freezing meat, poultry and seafood: See individual listings.

Thawing meat, poultry and seafood: Most cuts can be cooked frozen or thawed. Great care must be taken when thawing any meat, poultry or seafood products to avoid spoilage and deterioration of quality. Thaw them in their original freezer wrapping with a container underneath to catch any escaping juices, in the refrigerator. You do not want these juices to be transferred to other foods or work surfaces. (Clean exposed cutting boards with a hot soap-and-water wash, and then go over them with a mixture of two parts water and one part household bleach. Rinse.) These foods can also be defrosted in a microwave oven or by placing watertight packages in cold water. Remember that oxygen is food's worst enemy; don't leave any meat, poultry or fish uncovered.

— MEAT —

PORK SCALLOPINI

INGREDIENTS

1 large garlic clove, sliced
•
1 1/2 pounds very thin pork cutlets
•
Flour, salt and pepper
•
1/4 cup butter
•
1/2 cup chicken broth
(or half white wine)

Sauté garlic in butter over low heat. Remove garlic. Pound pork cutlets and dredge in flour mixture. Sauté over medium-high heat until lightly browned – about 5 minutes. Remove scallopini and deglaze the pan with chicken broth and/or wine. Add lemon juice if needed. Pour sauce over pork and serve.

SERVES 4.

One of the most popular uses for ground meat is the all-American favorite, chili. There are hundreds – maybe thousands – of versions that rate from so-so to sublime. Mine is served with Mexican Corn Bread, a great combination for a cold winter night in Alaska. I always make extra that goes in the freezer.

SAM'S JALAPEÑO CHILI

A pot of my friend Sam's chili, served to the Monday Night Football group of ten when it meets at his house, is always a hit. If you like your chili super hot, leave some of the hot pepper seeds in it and be prepared to call 911.

INGREDIENTS

1 pound *each* hot and mild Italian sausage, in bite-size slices

1/4 cup water

1/4 cup olive oil

2 cups onions, chopped

10 large cloves garlic, minced

2 pounds ground beef

3/4 pound *each* green and red bell peppers, diced

6-8 jalapeño chiles, chopped fine

12 cups Italian roma tomatoes, chopped

1 cup red wine

1/4 cup tomato paste

6 tablespoons chili powder

1 cup Italian parsley, minced

3 tablespoons *each* ground cumin and oregano

1 tablespoon dried basil

1 teaspoon fennel seeds

1 tablespoon salt

2 teaspoons freshly ground pepper

BEFORE SERVING

4 cups Italian roma tomatoes, in large dice

Fresh cilantro, chopped

Grated cheddar cheese

Green onions and tops, sliced

Sour cream

In a large skillet or stew pot, brown sausage in 1/4 cup water. Drain on paper towels and set aside. Cook onions and garlic in olive oil until soft. Add ground beef, stirring until browned. Add the jalapeño and bell peppers and simmer about 10 minutes until soft. Add tomatoes, tomato paste, wine and seasonings. Simmer for about an hour. Remove from heat and refrigerate overnight to blend flavors. At this point, freeze it or do what Sam does:

Before serving, reheat the chili and lay paper towels over the top to absorb any excess grease. After grease is removed, add chopped fresh tomatoes and cilantro, and simmer a few more minutes. Sprinkle green onions and a little of the cheese on top. Pass extra onions, cheese and sour cream at the table.

SERVES 10.

MEXICAN CHILI PIE

If you have all these ingredients on hand, this delightful supper dish is a snap to toss together.
TIP: To know what size baking dish will be large enough, measure the assembled ingredients.
Then see how many cups of water the container will hold. The results will guide you.

INGREDIENTS

1 pound ground beef

•

2 cups frozen onions, chopped

•

2 cloves garlic

•

1 28-ounce can tomatoes, or 3 1/2
cups, fresh or frozen

•

2 cups kidney beans, cooked

•

3/4 cups cornmeal

•

1 cup cheddar cheese, cubed

•

2 tablespoons chili powder

•

1 tablespoon ground cumin

•

1/4 teaspoon cayenne pepper

•

Salt and pepper to taste

TOPPING

1 1/4 cups skim milk

•

1/2 cup cornmeal

•

2 eggs, lightly beaten

•

1/2 cup cheddar cheese, grated

•

Salt and pepper to taste

Sauté beef, onions and garlic; drain off liquid. Add tomatoes, beans, cornmeal, cheese and seasonings. Cook over low heat about 15 minutes. Pour into casserole dish. Combine milk and cornmeal and cook over low heat until slightly thickened. Add remaining topping ingredients. Stir until smooth and spread over meat mixture. Bake uncovered at 375 degrees for 30 minutes or until crust is lightly browned.

SERVES 10.

CHILI WITH PORK AND PINTOS

INGREDIENTS

2 1/2 cups pinto beans, dried
(or 6 cups cooked)

•

1 pound *each* ground pork and ground
beef

•

1 large onion, chopped

•

1 green bell pepper, diced

•

2 large garlic cloves, minced

•

3-4 cups Italian roma tomatoes,
diced with juice

•

1/4 cup green chiles, chopped

•

1 jalapeño pepper, minced

•

1 roasted red bell pepper, chopped

•

1 1/2 cups fresh or frozen corn

•

3 tablespoons hot or mild chili powder

•

1 teaspoon freshly ground pepper

•

2 teaspoons *each* salt and cumin

If beans are uncooked, sort and soak overnight in water. Next day rinse beans, cover with water or chicken broth and cook over low heat until tender, about 1 1/2 hours. Add liquid if necessary.

In chili pot, crumble the pork and beef, browning until done. Lay paper towel over to soak up excess fat and discard. Add onion, garlic and peppers, sautéing until vegetables are translucent. Add remaining ingredients including liquid from cooked beans. Simmer at least an hour.

SERVES 10-12.

WANDA LaFLEUR'S DIRTY RICE

INGREDIENTS

5 pounds lean pork butt
or country-style ribs

•

2 large white onions, chopped

•

4 cloves garlic

•

Salt, cayenne and black pepper

•

3 cups white rice

Season the pork and cut it into very small cubes. Over a low fire in a large iron skillet, brown the meat in a small amount of fat. This is an unusual browning procedure because it takes about four hours. You will have a skillet full of hard, dark brown pork bits. Drain off excess fat. At this point add the chopped onion and cover the pork and onions with water. Again simmer very slowly, covered, until the water cooks down.

Measure six cups of water and add to pork and onion mixture. When it boils, add the rice. Cover tightly, lower the heat and steam the rice for 20 to 30 minutes. Chill.

SERVES 8-10.

BEEF NOODLE CASSEROLE

INGREDIENTS

8-ounce package medium egg noodles
•
1 pound ground beef
•
1/2 cup green bell pepper, chopped
•
15-ounce can tomato sauce
•
2 tablespoons tomato paste
•
2 tablespoons flour
•
1 cup *each* cottage cheese and cream
cheese, regular or lowfat
•
1/4 cup sour cream or sour cream
substitute
•
1/2 cup sliced green onions and tops
•
Salt and pepper to taste
•
1/2 teaspoon *each* garlic powder
and thyme
•
3/4 cup buttered bread crumbs
•
Parmesan or romano cheese

Brown the meat; drain. Add green pepper and seasonings. Cook 5 minutes and remove from heat. Add flour, tomato sauce and paste. Blend in cottage and cream cheese, sour cream and onions.

In a buttered 2-quart baking dish, lay half the noodles. Cover with half the meat-cheese mixture. Add remaining noodles; cover with meat and cheese. Combine bread crumbs and parmesan cheese and sprinkle on top. Bake one hour at 350 degrees or until bubbly.

SERVES 8.

— POULTRY —

The warehouse packs of flash-frozen chicken wings, breasts, legs and thighs are a boon to any cook and essential for ingredient cooking. Their availability in recent years at a lower cost has no doubt contributed to the fact that Americans today eat more home-cooked chicken. They are convenient, of excellent quality, and much less messy than dealing with a fresh chicken for many recipes.

Take care to avoid freezer burn after the package is opened, however. If you don't plan to use the pieces within a few weeks, wrap them individually in plastic film before repacking them in airtight zipper bags, or shrink-wrap. I know that's a bother, but who wants dried-out, tasteless chicken? Occasionally I buy another supply, forgetting that there is some left in the freezer. When that occurs, it is time to cook up a mess of chicken parts for future use. Freeze them in chicken broth for best results.

While cooks generally agree it's not a good idea to thaw and refreeze raw chicken, seafood and meat, there's nothing wrong with refreezing an item after it has been cooked.

Ground chicken and turkey are important ingredients in any number of combination recipes. Toss in some pasta, beans or rice, peppers, onions and seasonings and you have an instant casserole.

CHICKEN, BROWNED FOR THE FREEZER

Thaw frozen chicken parts in the refrigerator in their freezer wrap. To draw out any remaining blood, soak pieces in cold, salted water. Pat dry. In one or more large skillets measure butter, or butter and your cooking oil of choice. Figure about a half cup for the equivalent of two chickens. If you prefer, remove skin and fat. Sprinkle chicken with salt and pepper and dust lightly with flour; or, omit the flour. Brown over medium heat about 30 minutes, turning to cook all sides evenly. Sauté the dark meat longer than the wings and white meat. Cover the skillet and simmer another 20 minutes to tenderize.

Chill, wrap and freeze for use in dishes calling for browned chicken. Some that come to mind are *Coq au Vin, Chicken in Sour Cream, Chicken a la Contadine, Arroz con Pollo, Chicken Marengo, Chicken Cacciatore* and *Chicken with Lemon Sauce.* When preparing the final dish with frozen or partially thawed chicken, allow a little extra time for simmering the chicken. You may not save much time doing it this way, but you avoid the handling, frying odor and cleanup.

My sister Diane won a prize with her chicken chili at the annual Alamos Chili Cook-off, but I assured her it was only because I didn't enter this recipe – the local market had no black beans, a crucial ingredient.

While in Denver some years ago I heard a commercial for the Brick Oven Beanery. This chili was described in glowing terms. It sounded so good I called the restaurant and had some delivered to my hotel. The recipe came with the chili, a nice surprise. Both went back to Alaska with me, and friends were invited over to test the concoction. Cooked chicken is excellent in chili, especially in this recipe.

BRICK OVEN BEANERY CHILI WITH CHICKEN

The green peppercorns (preserved in liquid) are essential, but some of the other spices can be omitted or substituted without greatly affecting the outcome.

INGREDIENTS

5 cloves garlic, minced

•

3 cups *each* yellow onion and green bell pepper, diced

•

1 cup red bell pepper, diced

•

4 cups fresh tomatoes, diced

•

1 whole (3-pound) chicken, diced in 1" cubes

•

1/2 cup Masa Harina corn flour

•

1/2 cup olive oil

•

3/4 cup chili powder, hot or mild

•

1 1/2 teaspoon *each* cocoa, basil and oregano

•

1 tablespoon cumin

•

1/4 teaspoon *each* Tabasco, coriander and cinnamon

•

1/2 teaspoon *each* black pepper, cayenne, and white pepper

•

1 tablespoon green peppercorns, or more

•

2 cups V-8 Juice or bloody Mary mix

•

2 cups chicken stock

•

4 cups cooked black beans, rinsed

•

1/4 cup honey (you can use less)

•

Salt to taste

Poach the chicken in 5 cups of water for an hour. When cool, separate meat from bones and dice the meat. Return the stock to the stove and cook it down to 2 cups. Skim the fat with paper towel or fat separator.

If you're in a hurry, you can thaw frozen chicken in stock from your ingredient supply, about 4 cups diced chicken and 2 cups stock.

In the chili pot, sauté all the vegetables except the beans in olive oil. When soft, stir in masa flour. Simmer 45 minutes, then add black beans. Serve the chili in a large bowl with a scoop of rice in the center.

Accompany the chili with my version of Mexican Corn Bread. I prefer serving this instead of regular cornbread. You can bake the bread ahead of time and warm it, in serving dish or basket, in the oven or microwave. Leftovers can go in the freezer.

SERVES 18-20.

KATHRYN'S SPICY THAI CHICKEN PASTA

*My daughter Kathryn's housemates will do about any obnoxious household chore if she agrees to make their favorite dish.
One day she came home from work to find all the ingredients laid out on the kitchen counter with a big sign in front that read
"PLEASE MAKE ME."*

PASTA SAUCE

(Can be made a day ahead)

Heat oil in large skillet. Add garlic and hot peppers, sautéing about 15 minutes. Stir in other sauce ingredients and simmer. Remove from heat and add salt to taste. (If you are among the faint of heart, omit the Thai peppers.)

INGREDIENTS

2 tablespoons vegetable oil
•
6 garlic cloves, minced
•
2 jalapeno peppers, seeded and minced
•
2 Thai peppers, seeded and minced
•
1 14-ounce can unsweetened coconut milk (avoid watery brands)
•
1/3 cup creamy peanut butter (not with oil on top)
•
1/3 cup soy sauce
•
2 tablespoons *each* fresh lime juice and sesame oil
•
2 tablespoons fresh ginger, peeled and minced
•
3 tablespoons brown sugar
•
1 tablespoon honey
•
1 1/2 teaspoon Tabasco

ORANGE CHILI OIL

Peel the thin layer of orange skin from oranges and chop finely. Combine with other ingredients in non-aluminum 2-quart saucepan. Bring to 250 degrees on a deep-fry thermometer over moderately low heat, and let cook 15 minutes, stirring occasionally. Cool and let stand overnight in refrigerator. Keeps several weeks.

INGREDIENTS

3 large unblemished oranges
•
1/2 cup dried chili flakes
•
3 tablespoons fermented black beans, chopped
•
2 large cloves garlic, minced
•
1/4 cup sesame oil

CHICKEN AND PASTA

Marinate chicken in 2 tablespoons orange chili oil for at least one hour. Heat a large skillet until hot enough to evaporate a bead of water on contact. Add chicken and marinade and sauté until cooked through. Add bell pepper and onions and cook until slightly softened. Add pasta sauce and simmer while linguini is being prepared.

Cook and drain linguini in separate pot. Toss all ingredients together in the skillet and keep warm. Serve in large heated bowls garnished with chopped green onions.

INGREDIENTS

1 pound boneless, skinless chicken breasts, cut against grain in 1/4 inch strips
•
3/4 cup red bell pepper, diced
•
1/2 cup green onions, chopped
•
1 pound linguini

SERVES 4-6.

— SEAFOOD —

You can rely on the consistent quality of warehouse frozen raw fish fillets. They are individually flash frozen, hard as a rock, and kept at the perfect temperature. Once a package is opened, however, you should double pack the remaining pieces so that all air is removed.

Sometimes the warehouses feature fresh fish, shrimp or king crab at excellent prices. Take special care freezing these delicacies. Don't put too much in the freezer at a time or it takes too long to freeze, and keep the portions small. Double-wrap packages for extra protection against drying out.

If possible, cook fish frozen or just partially thawed and it will better retain its flavor and moistness.

DISHWASHER FISH

This recipe is included because I get many requests for how to do it. Being somewhat of a showman, I like to casually remove the fish from the dishwasher when dinner guests have arrived. Once, while hosting a reception for a Washington, D. C. dignitary, I removed and unwrapped a gorgeously decorated king salmon from the dishwasher, to the amazement of my guest of honor. He later sent me my favorite ham, a Smithfield, as a gift. In the accompanying note he asked for assurance that I did not intend to cook the ham in the dishwasher.

"Of course not," I wrote back. "As any good Southern cook knows, a Smithfield ham goes in the washing machine, on the wash and wear cycle." (Don't do this! I was just kidding.)

Lay a cleaned whole fish, 4-5 pounds, on a sheet of buttered heavy-duty aluminum foil. (With this method you escape the dreadful chore of fish scaling.) You can also do this with about 5 pounds of fillets. Completely enclose the fish in plenty of foil so it is watertight. Lay the wrapped fish on the top level of the dishwasher and set it for the hottest washing and drying cycle.

When the dry cycle is completed, remove the fish from dishwasher and unwrap or cut through the foil. Lift the skin off just the top of the fish – it will release easily. Place onion and lemon slices inside, and sprinkle inside and out with Johnny's Seafood Seasoning. I stuff in some sprigs of parsley, tarragon, celery leaves or chives if I have them. At this point you can also decorate the top of the fish with paper-thin lemon slices, sliced radishes, carrots or olives, etc. Rewrap, again watertight, and run it through another washing and drying cycle. Don't worry about overcooking the fish. The steaming process virtually guarantees against it. The salmon keeps it color, too. Test with a fork to be sure the fish is done throughout. If it isn't, a few minutes in the oven may be necessary, but that rarely occurs.

If I'm doing a fancy shindig, the fish is more likely to be decorated after its steam bath. Sometimes (well, maybe once a year) I cover it with a mayonnaise-based aspic and apply egg white cutouts for flowers, green onion tops for stems, etc. Use your imagination. Whatever you do, I guarantee you'll have fun with Dishwasher Fish.

KELLY'S LEMON-PEPPER HALIBUT

*Kelly Campbell, Alaska sportswoman extraordinaire, does marvelous things with seafood
she and her husband Jim bring in during stays at their McDonald Spit cabin.
You can't beat this super-easy way to prepare halibut.*

Spread tops of fillets with a thin layer of mayonnaise, regular or light, then sprinkle heavily with lemon-pepper seasoning. Broil over hot coals, on gas grill or under oven broiler for 10 minutes per inch of fish thickness. That's it.

GAIL'S RUM-BAKED SALMON

*Gail Phillips, Speaker of the Alaska House of Representatives,
prepares her award-winning salmon recipe on a gas grill.*

INGREDIENTS

King, red or silver salmon fillets
•
Dijon mustard
•
1 stick butter
•
1 cup brown sugar
•
1/2 cup high-proof rum
•
Salt and pepper

To prepare grill, set on low heat and place sheet of greased aluminum foil over grate, leaving space on sides of foil. Cut salmon fillets to fit. Lightly salt and pepper tops of fillets. You can leave skin on the bottom side. Spread tops of fillets with mustard and cook 5 minutes. Turn and cook another five minutes, then turn again. Grill lid should be closed.

Melt butter and stir with brown sugar and rum. Mix into a paste. After salmon has been turned for the last time, begin brushing the paste on the fillets. Repeat until mixture is used up, about 10 minutes or so for a 2-inch-thick salmon fillet. Keep lid closed between bastings.

For fillets of different thickness, estimate total cooking time at 10 minutes per 1-inch thickness of fish. Do not overcook.

GLENDA'S CIOPPINO

*My friend Glenda Rhodes quadrupled this recipe for our group of 18 women which meets
an evening a month at a member's home. We've been doing this for more than ten years,
an era of many memorable meals and good conversation. For such a large gathering, something in
a big pot is called for, and this cioppino recipe filled the bill. It was superb.*

INGREDIENTS

1/3 cup olive oil
•
2 tablespoons garlic, minced
•
1 onion, diced
•
1 pound mushrooms, sliced
•
1 green pepper, diced
•
3 medium tomatoes, peeled and diced
•
2 cups crushed tomatoes in puree
•
1 cup chicken or fish stock
•
2 cups red wine
•
2 tablespoons oregano
•
1 tablespoon freshly ground pepper
•
1 tablespoon salt
•
3/4 pound prawns, peeled and
deveined
•
3/4 pound steamer clams, scrubbed
•
3/4 pound mussels, cleaned,
beards removed
•
1 pound king crab legs, cracked and in
the shell
•
3/4 pound halibut (or other whitefish)
cut into 1-inch pieces

Combine the olive oil, garlic, onion, mushrooms and green
pepper in a large pot and sauté until vegetables are soft. Add
all the tomatoes, stock, wine and seasonings. Simmer for 30
minutes, then add seafood. Simmer another 5 to 10 minutes
or until fish is done and shells open.

This is a messy dish but so good. To protect guests'
clothing, have some nice dish towels handy to tie around
their necks. They will love sopping up the broth with chunks
of hearty sourdough bread.

SERVES 18 WITH LEFTOVERS.

CEVICHE, TWO WAYS

For an important event, this dish is a knockout. It can be prepared a day in advance.

INGREDIENTS

2 pounds halibut or flounder,
cut bite-size
•
1/2 pound shrimp, shelled and
deveined
•
1/2 pound scallops, cut bite-size
•
1 1/2 cups fresh lime juice
•
2 teaspoons salt
•
1 red onion, chopped
•
1 bunch green onions, minced
•
1/4 cup cilantro, chopped
•
2 tomatoes, chopped
•
1/4 cup *each* red and green pepper
•
1/2 cup *each* green and black olives,
sliced
•
2 bay leaves, crumbled
•
2 teaspoons chili powder
•
1 teaspoon oregano
•
1 cup dry white wine
•
1/2 cup olive oil

In a large glass container or plastic bag, toss the fish, shrimp and scallops with lime juice and salt. Refrigerate. The lime juice will "cook" the seafood in several hours. It should be white when done. Drain off the marinade and add other ingredients. Let the ceviche sit for several more hours in the refrigerator to allow flavors to blend. Drain off liquid and serve as a salad or first course.

SERVES 10-12.

Variation: Add chunks of cantaloupe, honeydew and watermelon just before serving for an even more spectacular dish. You might not think these ingredients would complement the others, but they do.

CHEESY HALIBUT OLYMPIA

This famous dish, presumably named after the Washington city, relies on two kinds of cheese that you should have on hand.
Any lean fish such as haddock, red snapper, sole, rockfish, perch or pollock can be substituted for halibut.
The other ingredients help guarantee that the fish won't dry out in cooking.
My friend Laurie Herman calls this her favorite "disaster-proof" company dish.

INGREDIENTS

4 frozen or partially thawed halibut
fillets, about 8 oz. each
•
1 or 2 sliced white onions
•
1 cup mayonnaise
•
1 cup Monterey jack cheese, grated
•
1 cup mozzarella cheese, grated
•
2 teaspoons (or more)
Worcestershire sauce
•
2 teaspoons lemon juice
•
1 teaspoon Italian herb seasoning
•
Salt and freshly ground pepper
•
3/4 cup garlic crouton crumbs

In a buttered baking dish (or use non-stick oil), make a bed of the sliced onions. Lay the fillets on top. Mix all but crouton crumbs together and spread over the fillets. Top with crumbs. Bake at 350 degrees until lightly browned, about 30 minutes.

SERVES 4.

CHILE SHRIMP DIVINE

I serve this almost weekly in Alamos where the prawns are huge and delicious. When the boats come in, the shrimp are iced down, carried in coolers and sold house to house. When Costco features similar fresh prawns on Fridays and Saturdays in Anchorage, I seldom pass them by and don't consider it an extravagance. Two prawns prepared this way are enough for one serving. You prepare the chiles, shrimp and bacon separately and then combine them for a wonderful taste combination. Be sure you have toothpicks in the cupboard.

The Chiles: Roast Anaheim chiles over a flame or under the broiler until charred. Put into airtight container to steam and then peel off the skins. Carefully slice the chiles from stem to tip in four strips, removing seeds. One chile is usually enough for four prawns, although sometimes they fall apart, so cook an extra one in case. Chill until ready to assemble.

The Shrimp: Put unshelled prawns single-layered in a skillet, barely covered with cold water. Add a splash of Zatarain's Crab and Shrimp Boil and simmer just until the shells turn pink. Plunge into cold water. They do not get fully cooked yet. Remove the shells (it's much easier partially cooked) and run a knife down the back to remove the vein. Rinse and liberally douse the shrimp with lime juice fresh or from the freezer. Chill until ready to assemble.

The Bacon: In one or more skillets lay out as many bacon slices as you have shrimp. The bacon should be sliced as thinly as possible and cooked about three minutes. It must not be crisp or it won't wrap easily around the shrimp. You can also do this precooking in the microwave. Chill.

To Assemble: Lay the bacon strips on a clean surface and put a strip of chile on each. Attach bacon and chile to the widest part of each shrimp and insert toothpick. Keep wrapping and inserting toothpicks as needed so the ingredients hold together for broiling. You'll get the hang of it after a few tries.

At this point I sprinkle the wrapped shrimp with a Mexican bottled sauce called Salsa Tetacahui. You might use Louisiana Hot Sauce or any of the popular new hot sauces that I haven't had the nerve to test.

A few minutes before serving, toss on a hot barbecue grill or under the broiler. They will be done in a flash, so be careful not to overcook. If desired, brush with butter and serve with lime sections.

CLASSIC CURRIED SHRIMP

This superb but easy dish, complete with its colorful trimmings, is all you need for a spectacular dinner party. (You may have to mortgage your house to buy the saffron, but the recipe really needs it.) Prepare the meal well ahead of the guests' arrival, and rest up for the occasion. The sauce, shrimp and rice are prepared separately, then combined just before serving. You can even freeze the cooked ingredients if you choose.

CURRY SAUCE

INGREDIENTS

1/2 cup butter
•
2 cups onion, chopped
•
2 cups Granny Smith apple, chopped
•
3 cloves garlic, minced
•
11/2 tablespoons curry powder
•
1/2 cup flour
•
Salt and freshly ground pepper
•
1/2 teaspoon *each* cardamom and ginger
•
1/4 cup fresh or frozen lime juice
•
1 heaping tablespoon grated lime peel
•
2 1/2 cups chicken broth (Tone's or Knorr's Gourmet Edge)
•
4 cups bottled clam broth
•
2/3 cup Major Gray's Chutney

In a large pot, sauté onion, apple, garlic and curry powder in butter. Cool slightly and stir in flour, seasonings, lime juice and peel. Over low heat add, stirring constantly, the chicken and clam broth. Bring to boil and simmer for 20-25 minutes, uncovered. Add the chutney and refrigerate until time to reheat.

SHRIMP

INGREDIENTS

4 pounds medium unshelled raw shrimp
•
3-ounce package dry Rex Crab Boil OR
2 tablespoons Zaterain's liquid Shrimp and Crab Boil
•
1 large lemon, sliced
•
1 large onion, quartered
•
1 1/2 tablespoons salt

In large skillet, barely cover shrimp with cold water; add remaining ingredients and bring to a boil. Turn off heat and let shrimp sit in the water. (They should have turned white on both sides.) Pour shrimp into a colander to drain. Remove the shells and sand veins, and refrigerate until ready to use.

RICE

INGREDIENTS

1 teaspoon saffron threads
•
1/2 cup butter
•
1 tablespoon salt
•
3 cups long-grain white rice, uncooked

Lightly brown the rice in butter in a large pot. Crumble the saffron in 1/4 cup of hot water and stir to dissolve. Add saffron/water mixture to the rice. Measure 5 1/2 cups water and add to the pot. When water boils, reduce heat and cover tightly. Check the rice after 15 minutes to see if water is absorbed and rice is tender. Cook a little longer if necessary. Serve immediately with the shrimp curry. Or, cook it ahead and, when cool, put the rice in a zipper bag and refrigerate. Reheat in microwave or pour into warm crockpot to serve.

CONDIMENTS You'll need eight or so small matching bowls for condiments that guests can choose from – the more the merrier. • Sliced green onions • Salted peanuts • Toasted pine nuts • Cilantro leaves • Chopped seeded tomato • Sliced cucumber • Pineapple chunks • Diced mango • Mandarin oranges • Raisins or currants, plumped in water • Banana slices • Chopped red and green bell pepper • Chutney

VEGETABLES

INTRODUCTION

Vegetables are a primary component of the "Eating Healthier" regime and, according to Supermarket Business data reported in *USA Today*, fresh vegetable consumption is on the rise. For the 10-year period ending in 1996, Americans spent 22% more on fresh produce. Canned and frozen vegetables saw just a 2% increase in sales volume from 1989 to 1997 in a survey by ACNielsen.

With the disease-prevention attributes of many vegetables becoming more widely accepted, consumption is likely to continue on an upward swing. In the last few years some excellent vegetarian cookbooks have been published, vegetables are being featured more often in food magazines, and restaurants have found bold, exciting ways to prepare and serve them.

At the warehouses, fresh vegetables are among the most popular food items, due in no small measure to their dependable quality. Produce buyers seek out the best varieties and sizes; and warehouse personnel are trained to treat them with kid gloves. Most vegetables are packed so well – and handled so little – that bruising or other damage is minimal.

Freezing vegetables: See individual listings.

Thawing vegetables: To maintain the flavor, nutrient content, texture and color of most vegetables, do not thaw before cooking. When vegetables have been blanched before freezing, you should allow less cooking time than for preparing them fresh. Still frozen, they can be cooked in or above boiling water, baked or microwaved. Thawed vegetables should be used quickly to prevent microorganism growth.

— ARTICHOKES —

Who can resist the warehouse packs of four bright green artichokes, each nearly the size of a large grapefruit? Not I, especially after a long artichoke "drought." Even if the tips or outside leaves are lightly tinged with brown, the edible part will still be good. Don't worry about keeping them fresh – they won't be around that long.

Served one per person, usually as a separate course – which it merits, this delectable vegetable has just one failing: only the base of each leaf is edible, not the entire leaf. Someday when I have nothing to do, I plan to scrape the pulp from all the leaves of one artichoke just to see how much there is. Probably won't equal 1/16th of a cup! But, then, there's still the artichoke bottom to eat after the leaves and choke have been removed.

Can you freeze whole artichokes? Yes. *Joy of Cooking* says put them into a pot of fully boiling water and blanch for 8 to 10 minutes. Immediately drop into ice water to chill. Drain and package in airtight zipper bags. To serve, cook the artichokes frozen or thawed about half as long as usual.

Caution: Once you cut the tips off an artichoke, air causes darkening. Dip in water to which a splash of vinegar or lemon juice has been added to prevent it. This same water can be used for cooking the artichokes.

If you'd like to try something other than the traditional butter, Hollandaise or mayonnaise with your artichokes, here are excellent alternatives.

ARTICHOKES, ITALIAN STYLE

INGREDIENTS

4 large artichokes
•
1 garlic clove, sliced, and sautéed in
3/4 cup olive oil
(or frozen garlic patty)
•
1 small jar capers and juice
•
Juice of two lemons and 2 teaspoons
grated lemon peel
•
1 chopped jalapeño pepper or 1/2
teaspoon red pepper flakes
•
1/2 cup parsley, preferably Italian,
minced
•
1/4 cup fresh basil, minced
•
Parmesan or romano cheese, grated

Spread the artichoke leaves and rinse well. Remove the sharp leaf tips with scissors (optional). Place in a large pot of enough boiling water to cover the chokes, adding vinegar, salt, peppercorns and a bay leaf for seasoning. Cover and cook for about 45 minutes or until a leaf can easily be pulled from the choke. Drain upside down. Meanwhile, make the sauce.

To the sautéed garlic add the capers, lemons and juice and jalapeño pepper. Simmer five minutes. Add parsley and basil. Do this much early in the day and spoon the sauce into a pitcher for reheating in the microwave. To serve, place warmed artichokes in four soup plates and pour hot sauce carefully into leaves. Top all with lots of grated parmesan or romano cheese.

SERVES 4.

STUFFED ARTICHOKES WITH MUSHROOMS

INGREDIENTS

Four medium-to-large artichokes,
cooked
•
3/4 cup Italian-seasoned breadcrumbs
(yours)
•
1/2 cup grated parmesan or romano
cheese, or more
•
1 1/2 cups fresh mushrooms, chopped
•
1/4 to 1/2 cup butter
•
1/4 cup *each* parsley and
green onions, minced
•
Salt and freshly ground pepper

Sauté mushrooms, parsley and onions in butter. Toss in breadcrumbs and remove from heat. Stir in grated cheese; then adjust seasonings with salt and pepper. Press the stuffing down into the artichoke leaves, sprinkling well across the top. A few minutes under the broiler, and a spectacular first course is ready. This mixture is also excellent pressed onto canned or fresh artichoke bottoms and broiled or sautéed.

SERVES 4.

—ASPARAGUS—

When the first crop of fresh asparagus hits the markets in Alaska, word travels fast. The 2-pound bundles from Sam's or Costco are a convenient size that can be eaten in a few days, and the quality is excellent. In season, asparagus is indeed a delicacy that quickly appears on dinner party menus and in local restaurants.

If the stalks look tough, limp, stringy and white, and the tips loose or black, that's the way many Alaskans thought asparagus was supposed to look. Happily, the shipping time has shortened considerably since those days, and you can understand why it is today such a coveted vegetable in the North Country.

In the early 1980s on a return trip to Anchorage, I was waiting anxiously in the airport baggage claim area for an entire crate of freshly-picked Number 1 asparagus, given to me by a California grower. The other passengers were astonished at such a magnificent sight. A big fellow wearing a Deadhorse, Alaska T-shirt walked over and drawled, "Ma'am, don't you know you're not safe in the streets of Anchorage with that?" I arrived home safely, but it was a long night blanching and packaging most of my treasure for the freezer.

An easy way to maintain fresh asparagus's quality is to wrap the stems in damp paper towels, without washing, and refrigerate in a zipper bag. If it becomes limp or a bit shriveled, place it in a tall container with a few inches of cold water. An hour or so in the refrigerator will revive it.

A favorite way to prepare asparagus is steamed in the microwave or on the stove, and seasoned with a little butter and lemon juice. Do be careful not to overcook asparagus; crunchy is good.

Even the tough parts of asparagus stalks, that you normally discard when cooking the more tender tops, can be put to good use. Blanch them for about three minutes in boiling water; then drain and toss into a freezer bag until you have enough to puree. The asparagus can be pureed, after thawing, with a little water or chicken broth-just enough to let the blender do its job. If you don't use the puree at this point for asparagus soup or as an ingredient for other vegetable-based soups, just pour into a jar and refreeze.

ASPARAGUS-STUFFED PROSCIUTTO

Spread thin slices of prosciutto with cambozola or gargonzola cheese. Barely steam medium asparagus spears (4" long). Wrap spears with prosciutto. Chill.

STIR-FRIED ASPARAGUS

Toss fresh or frozen (thawed) asparagus, cut diagonally in one-inch pieces, into many combinations of stir-fries. It adds taste, color and texture. Parboil fresh asparagus a couple of minutes first.

ASPARAGUS PROSCIUTTO BUNDLES

Another easy, do-ahead asparagus recipe: Wrap bundles of four steamed asparagus stalks (one bundle for each serving) with slices of prosciutto and lay them in a buttered baking dish. Sprinkle freshly grated parmesan or romano over the tops, then drizzle melted butter over. Bake at 375 degrees 10 minutes or until heated through.

ASPARAGUS SOUP BASE

INGREDIENTS

6-8 cups (1 1/2 - 2 pounds) fresh or frozen asparagus, cut in pieces

•

1 cup fresh or frozen white or yellow onion, chopped

•

1 cup fresh or frozen chopped celery

Simmer asparagus, onion and celery in water or chicken broth (from Tone's or Knorr's Gourmet Edge base) to barely cover. Cook until soft.

Puree ingredients in blender, adding just enough broth to blend. Chill.

Freeze in pint or quart jars, leaving an inch of headroom. To use, thaw amount needed.

CREAM OF ASPARAGUS SOUP

INGREDIENTS

6 cups chicken broth
•
4 cups asparagus soup base, thawed
•
5 tablespoons *each* butter and flour
•
1/2 cup milk or cream

In saucepan, heat butter and flour, stirring until lightly browned. Add asparagus soup base and chicken broth. Simmer, then stir in a small amount of milk or cream to taste. Season with salt and white pepper. (You can also thicken the soup with mashed potatoes, eliminating the butter, flour and cream.) If desired, garnish with croutons.

SERVES 8.

ASPARAGUS WITH CHEESE TOPPING

For this scrumptious asparagus dish, call on your supply of frozen asparagus.
It need not be precooked, since asparagus is always blanched before freezing.

INGREDIENTS

4 cups tender-crisp asparagus, cut in
•
1-inch pieces
•
1 1/2 cups breadcrumbs
•
1 cup freshly grated parmesan or
romano cheese
•
3/4 cup butter or margarine
•
Salt and pepper to taste
•
Milk to cover

In skillet, melt butter and add breadcrumbs to moisten. Beginning with crumbs, layer in baking dish with asparagus and cheese, seasoning with salt and pepper as you go. Top with cheese and breadcrumbs and barely cover with milk. Refrigerate until needed. Bring the dish to room temperature and brown in 375-degree oven 15 minutes. Note when seasoning: the cheese may be extra-salty.

SERVES 4 OR 8.

—AVOCADOS—

In Alamos, Sonora, avocados are important staples of the Sonorans' diets, and the locals know every trick for savoring and preserving them. While avocados are picked and shipped under-ripe in North America, in Alamos they are delivered daily ripe or near-ripe from local farms. The price is notably different: A neighbor recently bought a medium avocado for $2.49 in Tucson; she bought one the same size for 15 cents in Alamos.

The warehouse packs of four large avocados can be put to exquisite uses, but most likely not when you buy them – they are shipped unripened to protect them from bruising and splitting. You do the ripening part, scheduling when you want them ready. Store avocados at room temperature until ripe. Hasten the ripening process by placing them in a paper bag and into a warm cabinet – under the kitchen sink, for instance. As soon as avocados are ripe enough to eat, refrigerate them in zipper plastic bags. Some cookbooks indicate their lifespan to be only two days after that, but properly stored, they may actually last a week or more.

The other day a friend was making guacamole, and I was surprised to see her put a not-quite-ripe avocado in the microwave! I tried it (on medium power for 30-40 seconds) and, sure enough, it softened the avocado just the right amount.

AVOCADO PUREE FOR THE FREEZER

Until I knew avocado pulp could be frozen successfully, time and again I walked by the netted bags of huge green lovelies at the warehouse stores, wishing I could take them home. I knew a passable frozen guacamole was available, but it didn't occur to me to freeze avocados for it. So do it the next time you have a good supply – simple as one, two, three. One, peel and mash the avocado. Two, add lemon or lime juice to prevent discoloration. Three, pack in jar and freeze.

AVOCADO SALAD DRESSING

Mari Meyers, author of Gourmet Gringo, and a frequent visitor to Alamos, has made this dressing popular.
Prepare the dressing shortly before serving to hold off discoloration.
If made earlier in the day, cover the surface with plastic film and refrigerate.

INGREDIENTS

2 large ripe avocados
•
1/2 cup real or imitation sour cream
•
1/3 cup vegetable oil
•
2 tablespoons fresh lime juice
•
1 teaspoon fresh cilantro, minced
•
1/2 teaspoon *each* sugar, garlic salt and
chile powder

Spoon the pulp from avocados into a blender with sour cream or imitation sour cream, vegetable oil, lime juice, cilantro, and seasonings. Blend until smooth. Serve this dressing on any green or seafood salad.

SERVES 6.

CITRUS-AVOCADO SALSA

INGREDIENTS

1 avocado
•
1 grapefruit
•
2 oranges
•
1 tablespoon curry powder
(or less, to taste)
•
1 medium red onion
•
2 tablespoons green onions, sliced
•
1 tablespoon olive oil

An unusual and delightful salsa to serve with tortilla chips. A bit more work, but worth it. Peel and section one large grapefruit and two navel oranges, catching the juice and removing pith and membrane. Chop the sections, pouring the juice as it accumulates into a saucepan. To the pan add curry powder, stirring. Boil for about ten minutes, reducing the juices and curry down to about 1/4 cup. Cool and mix with the avocado, onions, and the olive oil. Walnut or vegetable oil may be substituted. Serve with tortilla chips and/or sliced jicama.

SERVES 4-6 AS AN APPETIZER.

GORGEOUS GUACAMOLE

INGREDIENTS

2 large avocados, peeled

•

Lemon or lime juice

•

Garlic powder and salt to taste

•

1 large tomato, diced

•

1 medium white or red onion,
chopped fine

•

1 poblano chile and 1 jalapeño chile,
chopped finely

•

Cilantro, minced

What better way is there to use avocados? Mash avocados and quickly sprinkle with lemon or lime juice to sharpen the taste and to prevent discoloration. Sprinkle with garlic powder and salt. Add tomato and onion, both chopped fine. Toss in a little chopped cilantro and cover the surface with plastic film until ready to serve with tortilla chips.

SERVES 8-10 AS AN APPETIZER.

CRAB-STUFFED AVOCADO

INGREDIENTS

4 medium avocados, peeled, halved

– FILLING –

2 cups crabmeat

•

1 cup celery, chopped

•

1/4 cup onion, chopped

•

1/4 cup green bell pepper, chopped

– DRESSING –

1 cup mayonnaise

•

1/4 cup whipping cream

•

1/4 cup chili sauce

•

1 tablespoon horseradish

•

Lemon juice to taste

Put one or two avocado halves on each plate, depending on number to be served. Mix crab filling with dressing and fill each avocado half.

SERVES 4 OR 8.

—BELL PEPPERS—
GREEN, RED, ORANGE, YELLOW

Few fresh foods are as versatile and useful to have on hand as sweet bell peppers. You can't do ingredient cooking without them. Even if a recipe doesn't need their zesty flavor, a few finely chopped peppers add color and texture to any number of appetizers, entrees and salads. Because they freeze and keep so well *without blanching*, buy them in quantity and set aside time to prepare them for your ingredient storehouse.

Costco and Sam's periodically sell bags of six peppers containing two each green, red and yellow, in addition to bags of all green or red peppers. Their quality is excellent – firm, heavy, smooth and glossy. Since they're not always available, I pick up several bags.

Last year I tested three cooked recipes containing either fresh peppers or peppers that had been frozen for nearly a year. My "guinea pigs" failed to notice any difference in taste or texture. (It's a good thing because I got the dishes mixed up and didn't know which was which. So much for a budding career in scientific research.)

So your counters are covered with 20 or so bell peppers that have been washed, seeded and halved. What next? Slice some; chop some, leave some as halves for stuffing, and bag them after fast-freezing on a cookie sheet. If you plan to use pureed peppers, wonderful in many popular dishes, now is the time to get that ritual over with. Besides, pureed peppers take up less room in the freezer.

Picture this knockout dish for a dinner party: A flat, rimmed serving dish filled with stuffed red, green, yellow and orange peppers. Try several stuffed pepper recipes until you find your favorite, then stick with that. A nice touch is mincing some of each colored pepper and mixing it with the filling of another colored pepper. A lovely contrast – not necessary but nice.

BELL PEPPER PUREE
(RED, ORANGE, YELLOW)

Lay halved, seeded red, orange or yellow peppers on foil-covered cookie sheets. Flatten peppers with your hand. Put pans two or three inches from the broiler and broil until the skins are mostly black and blistery. Remove with tongs to a paper bag or tightly-covered dish, and forget them for a few minutes. From this steamy environment, the skins and peppers will easily part company. Discard the skins. Pour any juice remaining on the broiling pans into the blender along with the peppers, and puree until smooth. That's all there is to it. Pour into pint jars, leaving an inch of headroom, and freeze until needed.

Fajita vegetable blend. Another trick if you are a fajita lover is to create your own fajita vegetable combination. For this you simply mix equal quantities of sliced white or yellow onions with red, green and yellow pepper slices, and freeze. Sometimes you can find a frozen combination of the three different peppers already sliced at Sam's Club – another timesaver.

Since this soup is a frequent must-have, you can bet there's now a good supply of yellow peppers in my freezer, and not at $2.99 each. It pays to be vigilant and to buy bell peppers at the best prices in summer so you can walk right by them, gloating all the while, when their prices skyrocket.

ROASTED ORANGE AND YELLOW PEPPER SOUP

This superb soup is made from pureed roasted yellow peppers and broiled oranges as the main ingredients. Once when I made it, yellow peppers were $2.99 each at the supermarket, imported from Holland. Because I had promised to serve this particular soup to friends, I gritted my teeth and paid $21 for seven of them.

The recipe came from the American Heart Association, and the only changes I've made are to add real butter and suggest some different milk options.

INGREDIENTS

2 large navel oranges (add extra orange juice if they are dry)

•

2 large yellow bell peppers

•

1 tablespoon margarine (or butter to taste)

•

1 cup chopped onion

•

2/3 cup grated carrot

•

1 tablespoon flour

•

2 cups fat-free chicken broth

•

1 cup 1% low-fat milk (evaporated skim, whole milk, or light cream)

•

1/4 teaspoon *each* salt, pepper and paprika

Cover cookie sheets with foil. Cut oranges in half crosswise. Place on cookie sheet, cut side up. Halve bell peppers lengthwise and remove seeds and membranes. Place pepper halves on cookie sheet, skin side up. Broil peppers and oranges until blackened, checking frequently to avoid setting the house afire. Put peppers in an airtight container to loosen skins; remove skins. Squeeze oranges to obtain their juice. Because orange and pepper sizes vary, I try to end up with the same amounts of each; that's when I sometimes add fresh orange juice. Put peppers and orange juice in blender.

Meanwhile, sauté carrot and onion in butter or margarine until soft. Add to blender and mix all until smooth. Refrigerate until ready to use.

To serve, combine flour, chicken broth and milk in saucepan. Whisk to blend, then bring to a boil over medium heat. Add blender contents and simmer for 10 minutes, stirring occasionally. Add spices to taste. Garnish with orange slices. (Somehow I've made this sound much more complicated than it really is.)

SERVES 8.

NOTE: For Roasted Pepper/Orange soup base, complete recipe through cooking carrots and onion; then puree in blender and freeze for up to one year. Freeze in pint portions. Do this when yellow peppers are cheaper; freezing just the base takes less room.

ROASTED GREEN PEPPER AND TOMATO SALAD

You'll like this unusual blend of flavors and different use of green peppers.

INGREDIENTS

1 large green pepper

•

2 ripe tomatoes

•

3 tablespoons fresh mint leaves

•

2 teaspoons olive oil

•

1teaspoon *each* lemon juice and grated lemon peel

•

Salt, pepper, ground cumin and garlic powder to taste

Roast pepper over flame until black and blistered. Place in airtight container to loosen skin. When ready, lift skin from pepper. Cut pepper into bitesize squares and put in serving dish. Peel and seed tomatoes and dice about the same size as peppers. Add to bowl. Toss gently with fresh mint, olive oil, lemon juice and grated lemon peel. Season with salt and freshly ground pepper, ground cumin and garlic powder. Chill and serve.

SERVES 4.

RED PEPPER SOUP WITH CROUTONS

INGREDIENTS

1/4 cup olive oil

•

1 1/2 cups white onion, chopped

•

1 tablespoon garlic, minced

•

5 cups (4 medium) red bell peppers, seeded and chopped

•

1 cup potato, diced

•

8 cups chicken broth (Tone's or Knorr's Gourmet Edge or from cooked chicken)

•

2 dried ancho chile peppers, seeded and crumbled

•

1 teaspoon salt, and freshly ground pepper to taste

•

1/2 cup whipping cream

•

Cilantro or parsley

Sauté onion and garlic gently in olive oil until onions are soft. Add remaining ingredients and simmer 30 minutes to an hour, covered. Add cream. Let contents cool before next step, or chill in refrigerator two or three days. Puree soup, several cups at a time in blender; correct seasonings. Meanwhile, defrost croutons. To serve, heat soup just to the boiling point and pour into eight heated bowls. Add sprigs of fresh cilantro or parsley and the croutons. The soup freezes well.

SERVES 8.

CHILE PEPPERS

How many times have you traipsed to the grocery in search of hot chile peppers for a particular recipe? Often the store is out of the kind you need or they're all shriveled up. If you keep a supply on hand, they seem to expire the very day you need them. Spare yourself. An easy solution is to buy a variety and freeze them whole in a jar. Or, you can chop the peppers, freeze them on a tray and then jar them. A salsa is not complete without a jalapeño or two.

Remember that both fresh and dried chiles carry their heat in the membrane and seeds, so scrape them out carefully unless you want a particularly spicy dish. Wash hands with hot, soapy water or wear protective gloves when working with chiles; they can really irritate your eyes if you forget and rub them. One squirt of chile juice in your eye and you'll wear glasses when working with the hot variety.

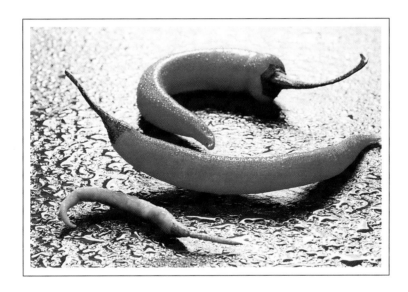

— BROCCOLI —

The large mesh bags of broccoli flowerets are a good buy, a cinch to cook, and full of Vitamin A. Be sure there is no yellowish color on the flowerets; they should be bright green. Broccoli keeps well in airtight zipper bags in the refrigerator, and if blanched a couple of minutes in boiling water, it's good for months in the freezer.

Steam it quickly; in fact, why not steam it right in the serving dish (covered) in the microwave. It keeps the color better. Don't add an acid such as lemon juice until after the broccoli is cooked; it can bleach the color out. If you want just the tips for a salad, pasta or stir-fry recipe, cut the stem part off after steaming and freeze it for other uses. Consider cooking broccoli ahead and warming it when company comes. That way the kitchen won't smell like broccoli.

Anchorage cook Susan Fison makes fabulous vegetable baskets to serve with various homemade dips. She puts fresh vegetables (snow peas, green beans, broccoli, Brussels sprouts, tiny unpeeled potatoes, carrots) in a colander, then lowers them into a pot of boiling water for just a minute. They then get plunged into an icewater bath. This extra step really enhances their color, and none looks as beautiful as the broccoli. With so many of us weight-conscious, it's always nice to have a low-calorie option for appetizers.

BROCCOLI SALAD

This is a tasty salad that livens up a soft-textured entrée.

INGREDIENTS

2 pounds broccoli flowerets

•

1 head cauliflower

•

1 green bell pepper

•

2 cups celery

•

1 16-ounce can black olives, chopped

•

1 pound fresh mushrooms, sliced

•

1 5-ounce can water chestnuts, sliced

•

2 cups cherry tomatoes, halved

•

1 package dry Italian salad
dressing mix

•

1 16-ounce bottle Zesty Italian
salad dressing

Chop into small pieces the broccoli flowerets, cauliflower, bell pepper and celery. Add drained, chopped black olives, fresh mushrooms, water chestnuts and cherry tomatoes. Mix together a package of dry Italian salad dressing and a large bottle of Zesty Italian salad dressing. Pour dressing over salad and refrigerate overnight. Sometimes I add a handful of crispy Top Ramen noodles.

SERVES A REGIMENT.

BROCCOLI PUREE

Broccoli puree is an ingredient well worth having in your freezer to add to soups or use for stuffing other vegetables. Simmer the broccoli in a small amount of chicken broth, then puree in a blender and freeze. Use some of your puree for this easy "souffle."

BROCCOLI "SOUFFLE" WITH SOUR CREAM

INGREDIENTS

4 cups broccoli puree
•
3 tablespoons butter
•
3 tablespoons flour
•
1/8 teaspoon nutmeg
•
1/4 cup sour cream
•
Additional butter to taste

In a skillet brown butter and flour to make a light roux. Stir in the broccoli puree. Season with nutmeg, salt and pepper to taste, and add the sour cream. Correct seasonings, adding butter if desired. Keep hot or reheat to serve.

SERVES 8.

BROCCOLI WITH WINE SAUCE

INGREDIENTS

2 pounds broccoli flowerets
•
1 cup light mayonnaise
•
1/2 teaspoon curry powder
•
1 teaspoon lemon juice
•
1/4 cup dry white wine
•
Roasted red pepper or pimiento strips
(optional)

Over low heat, cook the mayonnaise, curry powder, lemon juice and wine. Do not boil. In another pan, cook broccoli 6-8 minutes until barely tender. Pour sauce over and garnish with roasted red pepper or pimiento strips.

SERVES 8.

—CABBAGE—

There's no mystery to selecting a good head of cabbage; if its leaves are crisp and tight, and the head lacks brown spots, it will be perfect. Cabbage keeps for weeks refrigerated in a zipper bag, and it's always nice to have some on hand to serve steamed, fried or in salads.

One drawback of this hearty vegetable is its odor. You can do a couple of things here. Either put several large chunks of bread in the cooking water to absorb the odor or steam it ahead of time and immediately douse it with icy water. Refrigerate, covered, and reheat at serving time. Don't overcook cabbage; a few minutes are all it takes.

BARELY FRIED CABBAGE

Shred or chop several cups of cabbage and toss them into a skillet with a little melted butter. With the heat on high, sauté the cabbage for just a minute or so until barely cooked. Season with salt and lots of freshly ground pepper. Finish with catsup or sour cream to taste – just enough to give it some zip.

HAWAIIAN COLESLAW

People who aren't crazy about cabbage love this salad.
Proportions are not important, and you can be creative with the fruit ingredients.

INGREDIENTS

1 head cabbage
•
1/2 cup chopped white onion
•
1 grated carrot
•
2 cups fresh, frozen or canned
pineapple chunks
•
2 - 5 ounce cans mandarin oranges,
drained
•
1 1/2 cups raisins plumped in warm
water
•
2 small unpeeled apples, chopped
•
1 cup celery, sliced
•
Nuts, chopped

Start with 1 head of cabbage, part shredded and part chopped for variety in texture. Add remaining ingredients and serve with Hawaiian Dressing.

SERVES 10-12.

HAWAIIAN DRESSING

You may need to double this recipe, depending upon the quantity of your salad ingredients. Since the salad ingredients keep well, I usually do make more of the dressing. Supplement the pineapple juice with orange juice, if necessary.

INGREDIENTS

1 egg, beaten well
•
1/2 cup sugar and
1/2 cup pineapple juice
•
1 tablespoon butter

In a saucepan mix the egg, sugar and pineapple juice. Add butter and cook over medium heat until the dressing thickens. Pour over salad when ready to serve.

ORIENTAL COLESLAW

INGREDIENTS

1/2 head red cabbage, coarsely
shredded

•

1/2 head green cabbage, coarsely
shredded

•

1 each red, green and yellow bell
pepper, sliced and chopped

•

1 large carrot, grated

•

4 large radishes, chopped

•

4 green onions, sliced thinly

•

2 cups salted sunflower seeds

•

1 package dry Top Ramen noodles,
crumbled

•

1 cup jicama, sliced and chopped
(optional)

Mix all the chopped vegetables, Just before serving, add the sunflower seeds and crumbled dry noodles. Toss with Oriental Dressing.

SERVES 10-12.

ORIENTAL DRESSING

INGREDIENTS

Noodle seasoning
(from Top Ramen package)

•

1/4 cup salad oil

•

1/3 cup soy sauce

•

1/3 cup white wine vinegar

•

3 tablespoons sugar or honey

•

Mustard to taste

—CARROTS—

It took a while before I had nerve enough to buy a 10-pound bag of carrots from the warehouse. I neither had room in the vegetable bin nor the desire to walk around crunching raw carrots. Five-pound bags, for around $2, are sometimes available. The warehouse bags of baby carrots sometimes look dry, so I avoid those unless they are really fresh.

Select the bags of carrots that look firm, new and uncracked. They keep very well refrigerated in a zipper bag. If they get a little limp, soak them in icy cold water. To preserve their nutrients, scrub rather than remove the skins.

What to do with 10 pounds of carrots called for some ingenuity. I recalled a friend's serving bashneeps (that's what it sounded like, anyway), a dish from Scotland. Four large ones went into that recipe. Carrot and raisin salad, which keeps a while in the fridge, used another four. A few more were steamed and served with butter and mint. Several more were grated and rinsed with lemon juice to preserve the color, and these went into Hawaiian Coleslaw to be served the next day. The rest were prepared for my freezer supply.

CARROTS FOR THE FREEZER

In a large iron skillet, two pounds were diced, sautéed and frozen in zipper bags for eventual reappearances in pasta sauce, chicken pot pies, and casseroles. Another batch was sliced for soups and carrots and peas, and quickly blanched. Since blanching partially cooks the carrots, remember they'll take less time when they go back on the stove.

BASHNEEPS

Bashneeps is simply equal amounts of carrots and turnips cooked together and mashed with butter, salt and pepper, and thinned with a little milk. It is delicious, and a delightful change from mashed potatoes.

CARROT, RAISIN AND PINEAPPLE SALAD

This salad is always refreshing, and so simple. Mix it and chill.

INGREDIENTS

2/3 cup raisins, plumped in water or juice

•

2 cups grated carrots

•

1/2 cup pineapple tidbits

•

1/3 cup mayonnaise

•

1 tablespoon lemon juice

•

1/4 teaspoon salt

•

Optional: chopped nuts

Blend ingredients. Chill until ready to serve.

SERVES 4.

DOUBLE MUSKY CARROT CAKE

I am still searching for a human specimen who dislikes this luscious, moist cake from one of Southcentral Alaska's favorite restaurants, the Double Musky Inn.

INGREDIENTS

2 cups sugar

•

1 1/2 cups vegetable oil

•

3 eggs

•

2 teaspoons vanilla

•

2 1/4 cups all-purpose flour

•

2 teaspoons *each* cinnamon and baking soda

•

1 teaspoon salt

•

2 cups shredded carrots

•

2 cups flaked coconut

•

1 20-ounce can crushed, drained pineapple

•

1 cup chopped walnuts or pecans

Preheat oven to 350 degrees. Blend sugar, vegetable oil, eggs and vanilla with a wooden spoon. Stir in flour, cinnamon, baking soda and salt. Fold in carrots, coconut, pineapple and chopped nuts.

Pour into greased 9 x 13 x 2 inch Pyrex dish. Bake for 50 minutes, or until a toothpick inserted into center comes out clean. Cool completely. Frost.

CARROT CAKE FROSTING

Blend 8 ounces soft cream cheese and 1/4 pound butter until smooth. Combine with 2 teaspoons vanilla, 1/4 teaspoon salt and 3-1/3 cups powdered sugar, mixing with electric mixer until frosting is light and airy. Thin with milk or lemon juice as needed. Spread on cooled cake. Garnish quickly – before frosting dries – with pecans or walnuts.

—CAULIFLOWER—

Select creamy white, firm heads of cauliflower with bright green leaves. If cauliflower gets brownish spots on it, they can be cut off and the remainder is fine except for its appearance. Served with a sauce, no one would notice. My grandmother taught me to add milk to the cooking water "to keep its color and flavor," and I never argued with my grandmother! (Actually I did, and was on restriction for eight years.)

Cauliflower will keep longer if refrigerated in zippered vegetable bags – this may require cutting it in half to fit. It is best frozen as flowerets. Scald it first by lowering a colander containing the cauliflower into a large kettle of boiling water. Swish it up and down a few times to heat through (about 3 minutes), then plunge into cold water. Freeze uncovered on a cookie sheet; then store in airtight freezer bags. A very quick steaming is all the flowerets need before serving.

CAULIFLOWER PUREE

What to do with that gorgeous head of cauliflower that you planned to serve and didn't, that is beginning to turn brown on the tips? *Immediately* cook it and get out the blender. Melt 5 tablespoons butter per head and sauté some celery and onion in the butter. Put it all in the blender. Add just enough water or chicken stock to blend, then freeze the puree. The puree is the basis of a rich, tasty cream of cauliflower soup.

CREAM OF CAULIFLOWER SOUP

3 cups cauliflower puree, thawed
•
5 tablespoons flour
•
4 cups chicken broth
•
Nutmeg, salt and pepper to taste
•
2 cups milk

To cauliflower puree add flour and stir until smooth. Heat in saucepan and add chicken broth, stirring to blend. Add nutmeg, salt and pepper to taste, then gradually stir in 1 to 2 cups of milk. For a unique touch, add a sprinkling of chopped cilantro. Serve in heated bowls.

SERVES 4-6.

CAULIFLOWER WITH CHEESE SAUCE

For this quick and easy dish, break the flowerets off a head of cauliflower and steam for a few minutes in the microwave, until barely tender. Arrange in a single layer in a casserole. Cover with a cup of white sauce (2 tablespoons flour, 2 tablespoons butter and 1 cup of milk cooked until thickened) to which 3/4 cup Swiss cheese has been added and cooked until melted. Top with buttered bread crumbs. Brown in a hot oven (450 degrees) until cheese melts.

— CELERY —

The warehouse packs of celery hearts are tightly-formed, unblemished, and an excellent bargain. Can you walk by them without thinking of potato salad? Can you use all that celery, or will it go limp in the vegetable bin? Before getting into ingredient cooking, celery nearly always ended up that way in my refrigerator. It seems I would need a cup or just one stalk of celery for something in the making, then I'd forget about the rest until it was too late. But no more. Now I buy it with definite plans for its use.

The first thing I do is sauté about four cups of sliced celery with onions and garlic for tomato-based pasta sauce. Other ingredients may get added now or I might just freeze it as is.

Then I put on a pot of water that will ultimately turn into a nutritious vegetable or meat soup stock. Into the pot go the celery leaves from the first bunch (that went into the pasta sauce) and some additional sliced celery. An onion, 2 carrots, a chunk of frozen parsley, a bay leaf, a handful of peppercorns and some salt get added, and away it goes while I'm doing something else. Pour into quart jars for freezing.

Some can be braised with slivered almonds for tonight's dinner, cooked just enough to retain its crunchiness. Or I might cut it diagonally for a stir-fry with shrimp, peppers and snow peas.

If I'm still in the mood to be creative, I think about what kind of seafood is on hand, and another pot will be the beginning of a chowder with lots of celery in it. Or maybe cream of celery soup.

Oh, yes. I might even put some potatoes on to boil that will be destined for potato salad with lots of crunchy celery and onions in it.

I could also make stuffing for a roast chicken. And use some with the leftover chicken for chicken salad. Decisions, decisions.

Storage. Repackage your unwashed celery, once opened, in a zipper bag and it will keep up to two weeks. In the remote possibility that some of your purchase goes limp, all is not lost. It can be revived in ice water with a little lemon juice added.

Set some aside for chopping and freezing raw, and some can be sautéed before freezing. Toss the celery tops in a bag and freeze them too. Something I tried recently that I liked very much was pureed celery. I cooked it until soft, then blended it. The puree was frozen in 6-ounce paper cups and later added to potato soup and cream of asparagus soup for a different touch. It wasn't necessary to thicken the soup with anything else.

CAPONATA

*This is one of my favorite appetizer creations. It uses many of the same ingredients as ratatouille,
a very special vegetable dish.*

INGREDIENTS

2 pounds eggplant,
cut in 1/2 inch cubes

•

2 cups green bell peppers, diced

•

1 cup celery, diced

•

1 cup red bell pepper, diced

•

2 cups white or red onion, diced

•

1 tablespoon roasted garlic or 2 cloves
fresh

•

1/2 cup sliced jalapeño or pimiento-
stuffed olives

•

2 tablespoons capers

•

4 cups fresh tomatoes, chopped
(frozen or canned are OK)

•

1 cup extra virgin olive oil

•

1/3 cup red wine vinegar

•

1/4 cup *each* chopped parsley and
basil, fresh or equivalent

•

1/2 cup toasted pine nuts

•

2 tablespoons tomato paste

•

2 tablespoons sugar

•

Generous amount of salt and freshly
ground pepper

•

White wine (see directions)

Combine the olive oil, eggplant, peppers, onions, garlic, celery and tomatoes in a large skillet and simmer for about half an hour. Vegetables should be tender. Add all but pine nuts and simmer another 15 minutes. If vegetables get too dry, add a little white wine. Add pine nuts last. I like to let the caponata sit a day before serving (it keeps more than two weeks refrigerated) to let the flavors blend. Serve warm, at room temperature, or cold, depending on the weather and your menu. The caponata goes well with toasted French bread or hearty crackers.

SERVES A CROWD AS AN APPETIZER.

—CORN—

Forget everything your mother ever taught you about husking and scalding corn for the freezer. The absolute best way to freeze corn is to leave it in its natural-born wrapper. Toss the ears in a plastic foodsafe garbage bag and freeze – preferably within 24 hours of picking. You can also wrap the ears tightly in newspaper before freezing. Frozen quickly, I have had it actually be juicy as long as a year later. Sound unbelievable, but it's true.

Corn keeps a few days in the refrigerator in zipper bags, but the tassles should be removed to prevent stem rot. It is one of those high-moisture vegetables that could do better in the Ziploc vegetable bags with breathing holes. (See Part III.)

Try this perfected technique for cooking frozen corn on the cob: While still frozen, remove husks – easier done under running water – and silks. Rubbing the silks with a clean toothbrush opposite the way they grow is a neat way to get them all without freezing your hands. Cover with cold water and add a tablespoon of sugar. Cook, covered, just to the boiling point and let the corn sit in the hot water until ready to serve. Do not add salt, as it toughens the corn. If there's corn left over, leave it in the pot and have it cold for breakfast – it will still be juicy.

When a recipe calls for freshly scraped corn from the cob, bring some from the freezer, let it thaw enough to scrape, and you have your "fresh" corn. If your recipe calls for creamed corn, save the juice as you scrape it. If you're a little short on juice, add milk or cream to obtain the amount needed.

BEAUMONT INN CORN PUDDING

Corn pudding served at the Beaumont Inn in Kentucky, where I grew up, was one of the favorite dishes served family style at this popular restaurant. The inn may no longer be there, but I've saved the recipe and used it for more than 35 years.

INGREDIENTS

4 eggs

•

8 tablespoons flour

•

2 cups corn, grated from the cob

•

4 cups milk

•

2 tablespoons sugar

•

2 tablespoons butter, melted

•

1 teaspoon salt

Stir into corn the flour, sugar, salt and butter. Beat eggs well and add to milk. Combine the two mixtures. Put in greased 2-quart casserole and bake in a slow oven, 350 degrees, approximately 1 to 1 1/2 hours. Stir from bottom several times during baking. Sometimes I add a little chopped onion, and red and green pepper. You can also spice it up with chopped green chiles.

SERVES 4.

BAKED CORN CASSEROLE

Another good southern recipe you're sure to enjoy.

INGREDIENTS

1 pound bacon, cooked and drained

•

1 tablespoon bacon drippings

•

1 cup chopped onion

•

1/2 cup green pepper, diced

•

1 cup shredded cheddar cheese

•

2 - #2 cans creamed corn

•

4 eggs, beaten

•

1 can evaporated milk

Salt and pepper to taste

Sauté the onions and green pepper in the bacon grease. Put half the crumbled bacon and the onions and peppers in a large casserole. Sprinkle half the cheese over. Mix the corn, eggs and milk together and pour over the cheese. Add salt and pepper. Sprinkle the remaining cheese over this. Finish with crumbled bacon on top. Bake the casserole for 10 minutes at 450 degrees, then reduce heat to 325 degrees and bake another 25 minutes.

SERVES 8.

—CUCUMBERS—

The regular salad cucumbers from the warehouse stores – usually 6 to a package – are large, crisp and firm. Although I enjoy them, I consider the packages of three English cucumbers an extra treat. They are almost seedless, inexpensive, and have excellent lasting qualities, perhaps because they are individually shrink-wrapped at the point of origin. It's not necessary to peel them, another plus.

Cucumbers should be refrigerated in zipper bags to keep well over a week. Either variety can be used as is, although it is sometimes necessary to scrape the seeds from the regular ones. If they begin to get limp, soak them in iced salt water for an hour or so to crisp them.

Tossed green salads are natural allies of cucumbers, and they can be used liberally in many recipes. Cucumbers stand alone quite well, however, in these cold appetizer and salad recipes. The first one is a favorite contribution to the Friday evening get together of Alamos gringos.

STUFFED CUCUMBERS

INGREDIENTS

3 large cucumbers
•
1 cup small curd cottage cheese, drained
•
3-ounce package cream cheese
•
1/4 cup fresh tomato, finely chopped
•
3 green onions, including tops, minced
•
1 tablespoon mayonnaise
•
Freshly ground pepper and Mrs. Dash* to taste

Scrape the unpeeled cucumbers with a vegetable peeler if desired, or peel completely. Cut in 3/4 to 1-inch thick slices, which will stand up on the serving plate. With a small spoon or melon scoop, remove part of each slice's center to make room for the filling. Mash the other ingredients together and correct seasonings. The filling should be thick and not runny. Mound filling into each center and sprinkle with paprika or more Mrs. Dash. Sprigs of parsley can be used on or around the cucumbers.

*Mrs. Dash - A salt-free blend of dried vegetables, herbs and spices.

SERVES 12 AS AN APPETIZER.

JAPANESE MARINATED CUCUMBERS

INGREDIENTS

3 cucumbers

•

1 tablespoon soy sauce

•

1/4 cup rice wine vinegar

•

2 tablespoons sugar or equivalent
artificial sweetener

•

Dash of MSG

If cucumbers are thin-skinned, score the skins with a fork; otherwise cut part of the skin away with a vegetable peeler. Cut into paper-thin slices; then sprinkle with salt and let sit at least an hour to crisp. Rinse. Cover with other ingredients. Chill.

SERVES 4-6.

CUCUMBER AND YOGURT SALAD

INGREDIENTS

3 small or two large cucumbers

•

3/4 cup plain yogurt

•

2 green onions, tops included

•

1/2 cup chopped mint

•

1/4 teaspoon *each* ground cumin,
sugar and salt

Peel and slice cucumbers. Mix with other ingredients and chill.

SERVES 4-6.

CUCUMBER-ORANGE-ONION RING SALAD

This salad is lovely to look at and a great flavor combination. If oranges aren't at their best, I substitute canned mandarin oranges and get no complaints. Slice a red onion crosswise and separate into thin rings. Peel and thinly slice a large cucumber. Peel and slice three oranges crosswise or use 2 five-ounce cans of mandarins, drained. Arrange the rings and slices over bibb lettuce leaves. Serve with a basic French dressing or one with a few mashed raspberries added to it.

SERVES 4.

CUCUMBER SALAD DRESSING

INGREDIENTS

1 large cucumber, peeled and seeded
•
1 cup mayonnaise or plain yogurt
•
1 tablespoon cider vinegar
•
1 tablespoon fresh or frozen lemon juice
•
1 teaspoon ground chili powder
•
2 tablespoons green onion, chopped
•
1 teaspoon sugar and/or salt as needed

Mix all ingredients in blender, adjusting seasonings by balancing sugar and salt. Serve with iceberg lettuce salads.

— GARLIC —

For a pittance you can buy an abundant supply of this healthful, flavorful vegetable that, for years, had a poor reputation in certain circles. Garlic has truly gained respectability in the last two decades since ethnic cooking became popular and its healthful attributes known. The warehouses carry American garlic, which has papery white skin and a strong flavor. Feel the heads to make sure they are firm and unshriveled. To make life even easier, you can buy the deli jars of peeled garlic, but I'm partial to the fresh and don't mind the extra work.

Before developing the ingredient style of food preparation, my garlic heads would invariably dry out before I could use them up. In search of a garlic salvation project, I discovered an easy way to have fresh and roasted garlic without having to deal with it every time the mood hit. I keep some of each in the freezer. When working with fresh garlic, keep some baking soda handy (mixed with a bit of water) to rub on your hands to get rid of the garlic smell. Lemon juice works, too.

GARLIC PATTIES

For these wonderful timesaving flavor-injectors, simply sauté as much sliced or minced garlic as you want in one or two pounds of butter, butter substitute or olive oil. Ladle the finished product into muffin tins. When solid, toss the patties into a plastic bag and store in a handy spot in the kitchen freezer. You have just eliminated the chore of peeling, mincing, sautéeing, getting the garlic off your hands, cleaning the cutting board and washing the skillet every time you want a little fresh garlic taste. Your frozen patties will impart the same flavor as if you had done it ten minutes ago.

ROASTED GARLIC PATTIES

Unlike fresh garlic, roasted garlic has a wonderfully mellow, rich-tasting, nutty and far less potent flavor. You don't need one of the clay garlic roasters to do the job; heavy-duty foil works fine. Cut the tops off five or six whole garlic heads and drizzle olive oil over the tops. Wrap in foil.

Roast at 350 degrees until you can easily squeeze the garlic from one of the cloves. Do it too long and they dry out, so watch carefully – about 30 minutes should be enough. When cool, hold the bottom of the garlic head and squeeze the puree from the whole thing at once. Freeze in mounds on a cookie sheet or in a muffin tin, then package. How to use your roasted garlic? Serve it as the trendy restaurants do: mixed with butter or fine olive oil (and sometimes a fresh herb blend) to spread on toasted French bread. Or, for this fine recipe:

ROASTED GARLIC MASHED POTATOES

The first time I read a recipe for roasted garlic mashed potatoes, I was stunned that it called for forty garlic cloves. If you haven't tried it, though, you're in for a pleasant surprise. My usual assignment at family potluck dinners is to provide this dish. For my crowd this means about ten pounds of potatoes and eight to ten whole heads of garlic. Since you will have some roasted garlic puree ready in the freezer, this dish is just a few minutes away. Peel and boil potatoes. With electric mixer or potato masher, mix in milk, the roasted garlic, butter, salt and pepper to the consistency you prefer. For dinner parties, keep the potatoes hot in a crockpot or rice cooker.

ROASTED OR FRESH GARLIC OIL

Because fresh garlic flavored oils for salads or pasta can deteriorate and even become toxic, it's a good idea to make them in very small quantities, say, enough for two weeks. Often an empty spice jar is just the right size, especially for garlic-flavored oil. Prepared with roasted garlic, the oil keeps much longer; it is, of course, more mildly flavored.

—LETTUCE—

The warehouse romaine hearts (six to a pack) and iceberg lettuce (three per pack) last three to four times longer than the unwrapped heads from the supermarket vegetable bins, with good reason. They are shipped and displayed in their original packages and kept at controlled temperatures as long as possible. I have really been amazed at their "keeping" quality. Once you open them, however, repackage (unwashed) in zipper bags or plasticware, removing as much air as possible. A straw comes in handy for this purpose, or set the almost-closed bag in a container of water to force the air out.

CAESAR SALAD

This is the Number One salad at my house. Because the romaine keeps so long, I count on it for quick company meals as well as for my own enjoyment. The other reason is that it is such an easy salad to make.

Have all the ingredients ready – the romaine leaves washed and carefully dried, the cheese grated, croutons thawed, etc. Put a small saucepan of water to boil. Take an egg out of the refrigerator and put it directly in the boiled water for exactly one minute. Remove with a spoon, break the shell in a bowl and whip the egg with a fork. (For guests I have the lettuce and onions in the salad bowl, covered with plastic film, refrigerated. The other ingredients are in separate matching bowls, on the counter in the order they are to be added.)

Break the lettuce into bite-size pieces and toss to coat each leaf with the olive oil. Toss again with the beaten egg. Add onions and grated cheese, tossing. Add lemon juice, but not all at once. You don't want it too lemony. Season abundantly with pepper, lightly with salt. Last, toss in the croutons and serve immediately on chilled plates.

SERVES 4.

INGREDIENTS

3 romaine hearts
•
3/4 cup green onions
•
Juice of 2 lemons
•
1/3 cup olive oil with large sliced
garlic clove
•
1/2 cup grated romano cheese
•
1 cup garlic croutons
•
1 egg
•
Salt and freshly ground pepper

—MUSHROOMS—

You could paint a picture of the snow-white, firm, huge mushrooms that are standard fare at Sam's and Costco. The first time I laid eyes on them I was truly amazed and asked: "Why can't I get mushrooms like this at the supermarket?" It's not the mushroom's fault. They're nice and white until they spend time on the display counter. In contrast, the warehouse cartons are sealed, chilled and sold – just the way they were shipped. Leave them in the wrapped carton in your refrigerator until you first use them; then put more plastic film around the carton and they'll keep just fine.

The potential "warehouse" mushroom buyer still ponders the question: "Should I pay $5 or $6 for something I can't possibly use before they spoil?" The 3-pound cartons of Grade A mushrooms are truly a bargain, so it makes sense to have some idea what you will do with them immediately after they are opened. Here are some of those ideas:

Use fresh mushrooms liberally in salads, on a vegetable tray with dips, marinated, or in any number of spectacular casseroles and entrees. There is nothing that can substitute for the flavor of a mushroom, so it's wise to keep some on hand in ingredient form. You can freeze unwashed raw mushrooms up to three weeks. Lay them on a cookie sheet to freeze, then bag airtight for use in soups, stews, or for sautéing. Cook without thawing.

Sautéed mushrooms keep quite well in the freezer for longer periods. Prepare a batch or two for this purpose. Simply slice and sauté for five minutes in butter. Package in 4 to 6-ounce containers or as you intend to use them when thawed.

WALNUT STUFFED MUSHROOMS

INGREDIENTS

10 large fresh mushrooms

•

Stems from the 10 mushrooms,
chopped finely
(or use frozen duxelle)

•

1/4 cup walnuts, chopped and sautéed
in 2 teaspoons butter

•

3 ounce package of cream cheese with
chives (or fresh or frozen chives)

•

2 teaspoons lemon juice

•

Dash Tabasco Sauce

Put the chopped stems (or duxelle) in a nonstick skillet with lemon juice and simmer two minutes or so. Add cream cheese, stirring until melted. Add other ingredients and remove from heat. Let sit to blend, then adjust seasonings. Cover and refrigerate until ready to serve. Either microwave (on high, 3 or 4 minutes) or put under the broiler until hot. Serve from the pan.

SERVES 5 OR 10.

MUSHROOM PUREE (DUXELLE)

INGREDIENTS

1 pound fresh mushrooms,
tops and stems

•

3 tablespoons minced onions

•

3 tablespoons minced shallots

•

3 tablespoons butter

•

3 tablespoons olive oil

•

Salt and freshly ground pepper

•

Pinch of nutmeg

Wipe the mushrooms with a soft cloth or brush and remove discolored stem tips. Chop mushrooms finely. Lay some on a square of cheesecloth and twist to remove moisture, repeating until finished. Save liquid for adding later. Sauté the onions and shallots on high heat in the butter-olive oil blend. Add the chopped mushrooms and any reserved liquid, and sauté over medium heat until all the liquid is absorbed. Take your time doing this, because the puree should be very dark in color. When the color is right and the moisture has evaporated, add the seasonings and cool.

I freeze the puree in the smallest size yogurt cups, two or three tablespoons in each, then store in a zipper bag. The puree is wonderful mixed with rice, breadcrumbs, chopped sautéed vegetables or simply added alone to gravies, stuffings, sauces or soups.

The Cookbook Police will be after me for including the following "recipe" without being more specific. Truth is, I don't know how big your mushrooms are, how many you're cooking for, etc. So do as I do; improvise.

SIMPLE STUFFED MUSHROOMS

INGREDIENTS

Large, firm white mushrooms,
stems removed

•

Mushroom stems or frozen
mushroom puree, thawed

•

Butter

•

Bread crumbs, plain or Italian
seasoned

•

Green onions, minced

•

Lemon juice

•

White wine

•

Pecorino romano cheese, grated

•

Salt and freshly ground pepper

Sauté the mushroom caps in butter about five minutes, turning when lightly browned. Do not overcook. Remove from skillet. In same skillet, put a pat of butter, breadcrumbs, mushroom puree or stems, and minced green onions – estimate the amount you'll need to fill the mushroom centers.

Sprinkle with lemon juice and white wine. Season with salt, pepper and grated cheese. Adjust seasonings and press generous mounds of filling on the mushroom caps. Refrigerate until ready to serve. Put under the broiler for a few minutes to melt the cheese.

— ONIONS —

Besides being loaded with valuable nutrients and few calories, onions have long been credited with magic curative powers. (I recall, as a child, holding my head over a pot of boiling onions to cure a cold.) They've even been credited with giving the Egyptians strength enough to build the pyramids – and here I thought they did it by levitation.

We city folks are fortunate that farmers do all the work to grow such indispensable foods as onions, because they take a long time from planting to table. All we need do is pick up the sack, and pay for it. The 10 and 20-pound bags or boxes of large white onions, especially the Vidalias, are excellent buys at the warehouse clubs. Look for onions with dry, crinkly skins and no sprouts. Also available are bags of green onions.

Don't leave dry onions in the bag, and don't store them near potatoes – they gas each other to death. Weed out any soft, moist or dark-spotted ones, as they will spoil the others. Vidalias and Walla Walla Sweets are more perishable than the big Bermudas, but they all will keep much better with a little attention. That means giving them lots of air circulation in a cool, dark place.

I thought everyone knew the best way to store onions, but at my garage sale last summer, it was amazing how many people commented on the onions hanging by the kitchen door. You simply cut the legs off old pantyhose and use them to assure the onions get plenty of air circulation. Drop one onion into the foot and tie a knot. Repeat for each onion. Cut off the section that holds one onion when you need it. They'll keep much longer this way, and you don't have to worry about one bad onion spoiling "the whole darn bunch." Do the same with potatoes, and they will reward you with a longer life.

Here are some great ideas for making the best use of these delectable vegetables. Chop and/or slice several pounds of onions to freeze raw in quart-size zipper bags. (Spread them first on a cookie sheet so they freeze separately.) You'll want these handy for a multitude of dishes.

You can also put up a supply of cooked onions for adding to dishes containing pork, hamburger, cheese, eggs, chicken, seafood, and for relishes and chutneys. Sauté them for just a few minutes.

Onions keep well in your freezer and eliminate that trip to the grocery when you need them. Keep some in the refrigerator vegetable bin that you will use quickly. Cut onion is best kept in a covered jar or freezer bag.

Treat green onions, also called scallions, and shallots (small, roundish, aromatic onions) the same way, including the tops. Add them, frozen, to all kinds of vegetable dishes. I like to toss a handful of green ones in with other onions for taste and color appeal, and they are excellent sautéed in a skillet before adding fish fillets.

Slowly cooking sliced or chopped onions in a little butter gives them a wonderfully delicate but rich flavor for adding to your favorite recipes. This gentle cooking procedure takes half an hour or so; be patient until they reach a light brownish gold color.

If you have celery you need to use, sauté some onions with it, and freeze. You'll be surprised how many sauces, soups and meat dishes call for equal amounts of celery and onions to start them off. When a quick meal is needed, how nice it is to eliminate this chopping, sautéeing and cleaning up step.

EASY CARAMELIZED ONIONS

Restaurant chefs have a different way of doing this, but here's what I call caramelized onions. Partially cover a pound of peeled small-to-medium yellow onions with water and cook until barely tender. Remove from pan and let dry. In a skillet melt 4 tablespoons butter and 1/2 teaspoon salt; then mix in 3 tablespoons dark brown sugar. Add the onions and slowly brown them on all sides. They should be fairly dark but not burned – keep the heat low to prevent it. You can also chop the onions before putting them in the skillet – depends on how you want to use them.

Remember, an onion is a respectable vegetable in its own right, not just an ingredient. It can be cooked ahead and quickly reheated. Wonderful baked whole, or whole with stuffing.

ONION SALSA

INGREDIENTS

3 cups chopped Vidalia or other sweet onions

•

3 cups tomatoes, chopped

•

2 avocados, diced

•

1/4 cup cilantro, minced

•

Juice of two limes

•

Salt, freshly ground pepper and garlic salt

Serve with chips or as an accompaniment to roast meat.

BAKED STUFFED ONIONS #1

Cut tops and bottoms off large peeled sweet onions. Cut cone-shaped holes about an inch wide and an inch or more deep in each. (Size of the holes depends on the size of your onion.) Fill with stuffing such as crumbled bacon, cheddar cheese and buttered bread crumbs; or sautéed mushrooms, rice and Monterey jack cheese. Wrap individually in foil. Bake at 400 degrees until done, 45-50 minutes depending on size of onion.

BAKED STUFFED ONIONS #2

The first time I tried this, I overcooked the onions, and the next time I undercooked them. Sometimes it takes us a while to get things right. However, this dish is really worth the effort, as I told the hostess who served it surrounding a gorgeous beef roast. Can't think of a better way to use a good portion of one of those 20-pound bags of large, white onions.

INGREDIENTS

4 large onions, parboiled

•

1 cup frozen mushroom duxelle (yours)

•

3/4 cup tomato, diced

•

Chopped onion centers

•

1 cup brown rice, cooked

•

1/4 cup chopped pecans, toasted

•

1/4 cup green pepper, finely chopped

•

1 cup Italian-seasoned bread crumbs (yours)

•

Butter, as needed

•

Salt, pepper

•

2 tablespoons fresh parsley, basil, cilantro, dill or tarragon

•

1/4 cup Pecorino romano cheese, grated

•

1/2 cup red or white wine

As in the previous recipe, cut the tops and bottoms off each onion. Cut cone-shaped holes in each from the top down to about half inch from the bottom. Set the "holes" aside for the filling. Parboil the onions in water for about 10 minutes, watching to be sure they reach only the barely tender stage. Drain and set aside.

This is one of those "feel as you go" recipes. You begin with the basic ingredients, and add according to taste, texture and smell. If the filling is too dry, add butter, chicken broth, wine, or the water in which the onions were parboiled. Bake at 400 degrees 30-40 minutes.

SERVES 4.

—POTATOES—

Put a 10- or 20-pound bag of potatoes in your shopping cart without fear they will go to waste. When unpacking them, carefully sort and remove any that are bruised, exhibit major defects or are sprouting. Use these first. Cut off any green skin, as it can be toxic. Spread the others in a flat box or bin. Or, do it my way. Store the big baking variety in nylon stockings with a knot between each one. Takes five minutes and you have almost eternal potatoes. Remember not to store them near onions, as the onions will hasten their spoilage.

If you store potatoes in a bin, put an apple in with them, and the potatoes will last even longer without sprouting. When they do sprout, rub the sprouts off to buy yet more time. (These are not "old wives' tales.") Use older potatoes in a casserole for immediate serving.

If they've gotten a little soft, soaking in cold water helps revive raw potatoes. A 30-minute salted, cold-water soak before frying potatoes will also assure crispier fries. (Dry them well before frying.) Sometimes cooked potatoes turn dark – very unappetizing. Add a little lemon juice or ascorbic acid mixed with water to solve that problem. Cooking or reheating them in milk gives the same result.

Potato salad lovers should use new potatoes rather than the baking variety as they hold their shape better. Don't peel before cooking. In fact, there's no need to peel them at all – there's flavor and vitamins in the skins.

FREEZER BAKED POTATOES

For a handy supply of baked potatoes, scrub a dozen or so of similar size, rub them with butter or bacon grease and salt, and bake (not in foil) at 400 degrees until done. To reduce baking time, first let potatoes sit in a covered container of boiled water (but do not cook) for 10 to 15 minutes, or microwave for 5 minutes. After baked potatoes cool, wrap individually and freeze. Heat in the oven frozen or thawed. Leftover baked potatoes are great diced or sliced and browned in a skillet with scrambled eggs added.

If microwaving your bakers, pierce them with a fork first and lay them in a ring on paper toweling to absorb moisture. They should all be uniform in size and shape to cook evenly.

Mashed, whipped, fried or twice-baked potatoes all freeze well. Potatoes frozen in soups, stews and casseroles don't fare as well as they tend to get mushy.

MASHED POTATOES AND GRAVY

It is an unpardonable sin to waste good gravy on instant potatoes. With the fresh variety so inexpensive, tasty and quick to prepare, why settle for boring instant? Peel and quarter or slice potatoes, and put them, barely covered with water, in a saucepan. Cover and cook about 10 minutes or until easily pierced with a fork. Drain the water into another container. (It can be saved for soup stock or bread baking.) Add a small amount of milk or cream, butter, salt and pepper to the potatoes and put the pan back on the stove over low heat.

Mash the mixture first with a potato masher, then beat with a hand mixer. Add more milk or some of the reserved potato water, but don't get carried away; the potatoes should be hearty and dense, not light. If you add too much liquid, they will be watery when served. Transfer potatoes to heated container or keep warm in a microwave oven. For gravy, see Gravy listing.

For *Roasted Garlic Mashed Potatoes* see Garlic listing.

To keep mashed potatoes hot for a dinner party, serve them from an electric crockpot or rice cooker. Also, coffee carafes do double duty for keeping gravy and sauces hot for hours. (Soak the carafe beforehand with baking soda and water to remove coffee flavor.) When gravy is ready, fill the pot with very hot water, then pour it out, replacing it with hot gravy. Be sure to put the carafe to soak after serving the gravy; it will be easier to clean.

BAKED POTATO SKINS

A favorite appetizer at my house is baked potato skins. Neatly remove most of the pulp from chilled baked potatoes, preferably yesterday's. Cut into quarters lengthwise and sprinkle the insides with Cajun seasoning. Quick-fry in very hot oil, drain thoroughly on paper towels and serve with or without a dipping sauce.

Or, sprinkle cut potatoes with olive oil, salt and pepper, and brown them, cut side up on a cookie sheet, in a 475-degree oven. If that's not spicy enough for your tastes, top the potatoes with chopped tomato, grated sharp cheddar cheese, sliced jalapeño peppers, and chopped green onions.

Back to the hot oven to melt the cheese, then serve with real or imitation sour cream.

You will have some leftover pulp on hand from your baked potato skins. Don't throw it away. Use it to thicken soups and gravies, for making mashed potatoes, and for potato cakes. Or you can crumble the potato, fry it with onions and peppers and add some eggs for a great omelet.

BAKED POTATOES AND ONIONS

For each serving, slice 1 white onion crosswise into 4 or 5 slices and 1 baking potato (skin on) of the same diameter. Dredge each onion slice in freshly grated parmesan or romano cheese and alternate it between the potato slices. Spray a sheet of aluminum foil with butter flavoring and place the reassembled potato-onion on it. Sprinkle more cheese on exposed side, and salt and pepper. Fold the foil tightly and bake about an hour at 350-375 degrees. A different accompaniment to a light entrée, but impressive. Vary with crumbled bacon, cheddar cheese or parsley and paprika between the layers.

—SPINACH—

Buy the 2 1/2 pound bag of prewashed, stemmed spinach, making sure it is all green, with no dark, slimy leaves. Granted, it looks like a lot of spinach, especially if you're cooking for one, but think what you can do with it! Even though it's prewashed, I rinse it again in a sink full of water. Drain and package part of the fresh spinach for salads, refrigerating in a zipper bag.

The rest of it can be steamed for later use. To steam spinach, stuff it into a large covered pot with no added water, being careful not to overcook. About five minutes will do it. Watch it shrink down to practically nothing! (Makes one appreciate the price of frozen spinach.) Chop or leave whole. What you don't eat you can freeze in quart-size zipper bags.

GARLIC SPINACH

A simple but superb way to serve spinach is to sauté several garlic cloves in butter until lightly browned. Add fresh spinach, salt, pepper and a little fresh lemon; cover and steam for several minutes.

SPINACH, SCALLOP
AND MUSHROOM SALAD

This is a warm salad, perfect for spur-of-the-moment company.
Because I try to have fresh spinach and mushrooms on hand most of the time, I buy the scallops to go with them.
One pound of scallops gets sliced and packed in small jars for the freezer. The salad doesn't require very many.
The onions, gingerroot, pine nuts and garlic/olive oil cube can also be from your freezer supply.

INGREDIENTS

6-8 cups spinach leaves
•
1 tablespoon *each* rice vinegar and
dry sherry
•
6 ounces scallops
•
2 tablespoons green onions, sliced
•
1 garlic clove
•
1 teaspoon ginger root, shredded
•
3 tablespoons olive oil
•
Salt and pepper
•
Pine nuts (optional)

Place spinach leaves in a large bowl. Add some sliced, white fresh mushrooms. Toss with rice vinegar and dry sherry. Set aside or chill.

Just before serving, sauté scallops in a skillet (slice them if they are large) with sliced green onions, a garlic clove, gingerroot and olive oil. Cook a minute or two until scallops turn opaque. Pour hot scallop mixture over spinach in bowl and toss. Season with salt and pepper. Arrange the wilted spinach on salad plates and sprinkle with toasted pine nuts.

SERVES 4.

SWEET AND SOUR SPINACH SALAD

*My Portland, Oregon, friend Kris Goodrich serves this salad with canned mandarin oranges
when she's in a hurry. Try it both ways.*

INGREDIENTS

1 1/2 pounds fresh spinach

•

1 medium or small red onion

•

2 oranges

•

3 tablespoons sugar

•

1/4 cup cider vinegar

•

1/2 teaspoon *each* dry mustard,
paprika and salt

•

1/2 cup olive or salad oil

Place spinach leaves in a serving bowl with a small red onion separated into rings. Chill. Peel oranges and slice crosswise, removing any noticeable membrane. In a jar, mix sugar, cider vinegar and the spices. Stir. Add salad oil or olive oil and shake until well blended. Toss with spinach before adding orange slices, then lightly afterward. Serve.

Other good things to add: Toasted pine nuts, shredded jicama, strawberries, cucumber slices, mashed egg yolks – use your imagination.

SERVES 4-6.

CHEESY SPINACH

INGREDIENTS

3 packed cups of frozen or fresh
spinach, cooked

•

1/4 cup sour cream

•

1 tablespoon grated onion

•

2 tablespoons lemon juice

•

1/2 teaspoon *each* salt and sugar

•

1/2 cup Roquefort or blue cheese

•

3 ounces cream cheese

In saucepan on stove or serving dish in microwave, cook the spinach. Add the remaining ingredients and heat thoroughly, stirring to blend.

SERVES 4.

SPINACH PASTA CASSEROLE

INGREDIENTS

12-ounce package of pasta rings,
shells or wheels, cooked, drained

•

3 cups fresh spinach, chopped,
OR
2 10-ounce packages frozen chopped
spinach

•

2 cups sour cream

•

1 cup green chiles, diced

•

1/4 cup lemon juice

•

1/4 cup onion, chopped

•

2 teaspoons dill weed

•

1 1/2 teaspoons garlic salt

•

2 cups mozzarella cheese, shredded

•

1 1/2 cups crushed tortilla chips from
package

•

1 medium avocado, sliced

•

1 tomato, wedged

•

6 sliced black olives

Combine cooked pasta with spinach. Blend sour cream, chiles, lemon juice, onion, dill and garlic salt. Alternate layers of pasta-spinach mixture with sour cream mixture. Sprinkle cheese over and top with tortilla chips, avocado, tomato and olives. Heat in 350-degree oven until hot and cheese melts.

SERVES 6-8.

—TOMATOES—

"Cardboard" tomatoes – that's what Alaskans are used to, picked and shipped way too soon, with the taste and texture of, you guessed it, cardboard. Truth is, tomatoes can't survive the trip if they are ripe, so we often settle for what looks like a tomato. After a years-long quest for the vine-ripened flavor of Kentucky tomatoes, I tried placing a fluorescent fixture under an overhead kitchen cabinet with a Gro-Lux light. Wonder of wonders, the tomatoes ripened nicely, and the flavor improved considerably! (Fruit on my counter is ripened this way, too.)

The flats of tomatoes at Costco and Sam's are a joy to behold. If you spot an imperfect specimen, substitute one from another case. This goes for any case goods, incidentally. Store personnel seldom frown on this practice – they'd rather have satisfied members. You'll note any overripe or bruised items are periodically removed from the display area.

Buy a flat, and let them ripen at room temperature, refrigerating only if necessary. Once refrigerated, take them out an hour or so before serving to refresh the flavor. Use fresh in sandwiches, salads, salsas, soups or iced gazpacho. Or, try them sliced and broiled atop a slice of cheddar cheese on toast.

Broil a few with the tops cut off, sprinkled with a simple butter-cheese-breadcrumb topping. You should have some left for these favorite recipes that always bring raves for the cook: Fresh Tomato Pasta Sauce; Okra, Corn and Tomatoes; Spanish Rice; and Fresh Tomato Soup.

Italian (roma) tomatoes have an intense flavor and color, less juice and fewer seeds than ordinary varieties. For these reasons, they work especially well in tossed salads. Drain juicy tomatoes on paper toweling before adding them, last, to salads. Or, put them in your salad bowl and keep off to the side. Soak up any juice with paper towel before tossing salad.

TOMATO SALSA

INGREDIENTS

5 or 6 firm, ripe tomatoes, chopped
(about 4 cups)

•

3/4 to 1 cup chopped fresh or frozen
green, red or white onions (or
combination)

•

1 large clove garlic, minced

•

1/4 cup cilantro, minced

•

1 or 2 fresh or frozen Anaheim chiles
(poblanos) minced

•

1 or 2 fresh or frozen jalapeño chiles,
minced

•

1 tablespoon *each* olive oil and fresh or
frozen lemon or lime juice

•

Salt and freshly ground pepper to taste

Chop the tomatoes separately, then the onions. Put the other vegetables on the cutting board and mince. Add seasonings, cover and chill. Pass the tortilla chips.

SERVES 8 TO 10.

SUPREME FRESH TOMATO PASTA SAUCE

No matter what variations I make to a tomato-based pasta sauce, it always starts out the same – with sautéed garlic, celery, carrot, bell pepper and onion. This recipe must be good; friends invite themselves over for it, including those of Italian origin, who keep coming back for more. This is a difficult recipe to quantify, because I am not careful at all with the measurements. You needn't be careful, either; it will taste just as good with a little more or less of each ingredient. What is important, though, is slowly sautéing the vegetables.

I'll give you ingredients for a large pot since the sauce is so handy to have in the freezer. A note about the cheese to be served with the sauce and pasta. I used to order Pecorino romano, a marvelous grating cheese, shipped from the East Coast to Alaska. You can imagine our excitement to find it in Anchorage, at our Costco store! In true Italian-style, it must be grated feather-light. Zyliss makes one of the best graters for this purpose, a small plastic version.

INGREDIENTS

2 large garlic cloves, sliced

•

2 cups *each* green bell pepper, onions, celery, chopped

•

1/2 cup *each* fresh herbs (basil, oregano, thyme, parsley, minced)
OR
3 tablespoons Tone's or McCormick spaghetti sauce seasoning

•

5 pounds chopped tomatoes, regular or roma, and juice

•

1 16-ounce can each tomato sauce and tomato paste

•

Salt, pepper and cayenne pepper to taste

•

One or two bay leaves (remove later)

•

Fresh mushrooms, sliced

•

1 cup good red table wine

Sauté garlic in olive oil, then add vegetables and fresh herbs or seasoning. When vegetables are soft, add tomatoes, sauce and tomato paste; then add remaining ingredients. (Mushrooms and wine can be added just before serving if cooking the sauce ahead.)

Simmer about an hour, then cool to give flavors a chance to blend. Taste by dipping bread in the sauce. If too tart, add a small amount of sugar.

Secret Ingredient: Freshly grated Pecorino romano (from the warehouse deli section), truly a superb cheese to pass with the sauce.

SERVES A CROWD.

FRESH TOMATO SOUP

INGREDIENTS

6 large ripe tomatoes, diced

•

2 tablespoons tomato paste

•

4 cups chicken broth (Tone's or Knorr's Gourmet Edge chicken base, reconstituted)

•

11/2 cups fresh or frozen white onion, chopped

•

1/2 cup green bell pepper (or 1/4 each green and red), chopped

•

1 stalk celery, chopped

•

1 large carrot, chopped fine

•

1 large clove garlic, minced

•

2-4 tablespoons Bertolli olive oil

•

Salt, freshly ground pepper and sugar to taste

•

Few leaves *each* fresh basil, oregano, parsley or cilantro, minced

•

Milk or cream, optional

•

1 tablespoon butter, optional

•

Garlic croutons, served separately

Sauté onion, celery, bell pepper, carrot and garlic in olive oil until soft. Add, and cook until soft, tomatoes and tomato paste. Mix chicken base with water and add to pan. Simmer at least 30 minutes with herbs and seasonings. Taste and adjust seasonings, then pour the ingredients into a blender, mixing until smooth.

When ready to serve, reheat the soup. At this point, you may wish to add a small amount of milk or cream and butter for a mellower flavor. Serve with garlic croutons (see recipe).

SERVES 12.

TABOULI SALAD

Why restaurants can't serve a decent tabouli is a mystery to me. It's such a simple, straightforward dish, and so wonderful. Still, no one can make it like my Aunt Mimi. She chops everything superfine.

sINGREDIENTS

2 bunches parsley, chopped

•

2 bunches mint, chopped

•

4 tomatoes, chopped small

•

2 cucumbers, chopped small

•

2 bunches green onions with tops, minced

•

1 1/4 cups berghul (bulgur wheat), washed

•

Lemon juice, see directions

•

Olive oil, see directions

•

Salt and freshly ground pepper

•

Allspice, pinch

In a mixing bowl, cover berghul with water and let stand for 30 minutes to absorb the water. Squeeze out excess water. After chopping all the vegetables finely, mix them with the berghul. To dress the salad, sprinkle 1/4 cup olive oil and 1/4 cup lemon juice over it. Mix and add spices. At this point begin tasting – it will probably need more olive oil and lemon juice. Let stand for one or two hours before serving, chilled.

NOTE: Tabouli may be served with fresh romaine leaves that are used to scoop up the salad.

SERVES 8-10.

BROILED TOMATOES WITH CHEESE AND SHERRY

INGREDIENTS

Large firm tomatoes, halved

•

Salt, pepper, oregano

•

Mayonnaise (1/2 to 1 tablespoon per tomato half)

•

Grated parmesan cheese

•

Dry sherry

Lay the desired number of tomato halves on a cookie sheet or baking dish, cut side up. Sprinkle each with sherry, then salt, pepper and oregano to taste. Put dollop of mayonnaise on each one and cover with grated cheese. Place under oven broiler to brown, but be careful not to overcook tomatoes.

OKRA, CORN AND TOMATOES, SOUTHERN STYLE

The last time I served this family favorite to company, two of the guests went to the kitchen before dessert and fought over the remainder in the dish. This is such a pleasing vegetable combination – I'm surprised it isn't served more often. Yes, it takes a while to sauté all the ingredients – which is why I make such a large quantity when fresh tomatoes and corn are available. Another plus is its combination of colors that brightens any menu.

The finished product gets divided into two portions (each serving about 10) and placed in two foil or plastic film-lined serving dishes headed for the freezer. When the okra, corn and tomato mixture is solidly frozen, I remove the bowls from the contents so they can be used for other purposes. The mixture keeps six months to a year. When ready to use, remove the wrapping and return to the serving dish to be thawed and reheated in the microwave.

INGREDIENTS

4 cups fresh or frozen okra (thawed), cut into 1/2 inch slices

•

4 cups fresh corn, scraped from cob, or frozen

•

4 cups fresh tomatoes, chopped into 1/2 inch squares

•

1 bunch fresh or frozen green onions or 1 cup white onion, chopped

•

4 tablespoons butter

•

1 fresh or frozen jalapeño pepper, seeded and minced

•

1/2 cup fresh or frozen green bell pepper, chopped

•

Salt and freshly ground pepper to taste

•

Lemon juice (if necessary)

Melt 2 tablespoons of the butter in large skillet. On medium-high, cook and stir okra, lifting with spatula as it begins to brown and lose its unpopular, slimy texture. Fry until nicely browned and dry, about 15 minutes. Scrape from pan into large bowl. Put peppers and corn into same pan with remaining butter. If corn is milky, fry until liquid is absorbed. Season to taste and add to okra in bowl. Sauté the tomatoes with the onions until soft and add to other ingredients, tossing well. Divide into two portions, one for immediate use or both for the freezer as described above. One last note: Just before serving, correct the seasoning with lemon if it seems a bit too sweet.

MAKES TWO CASSEROLES SERVING 10 EACH.

THE WORLD'S BEST GAZPACHO

I can say this after having tested more than 50 gazpacho recipes in the last two decades – besides, this is my book. Also, I can say, authoritatively, that there are only three people on the North American continent who don't like it. Therefore you can trust me when I say gazpacho is a very safe, popular dinner party dish. It is also great for weight-loss diets. It keeps for days, covered, in the refrigerator.

What is it? A soup. A salad. Both actually, and best served icy cold. Here is a guaranteed-to-please version. Promise me, though, that you will not resort to mechanical means of any kind to chop the vegetables. Reddish slush is not what we are striving for.

INGREDIENTS

1 cup fresh or frozen white onion, chopped

•

1 teaspoon minced garlic

•

2 cups fresh green pepper, chopped

•

4-5 cups fresh tomato, chopped

•

2 medium-sized cucumbers, seeded and chopped

•

1 whole bunch parsley, chopped

•

2 1/2 cups water or mildly flavored chicken broth

•

2 1/2 cups Bloody Mary Mix (any brand)

•

1/2 to 3/4 cup fresh or frozen lemon juice

•

1/3 cup fruity olive oil

•

1/2 tablespoon *each* salt and freshly ground pepper

•

1 tablespoon paprika

•

Garlic croutons

Chop tomatoes, sliding them and their juice into glass mixing bowl. Finely chop remaining vegetables together on large cutting board, but keep them large enough to be identifiable. The soup should look wonderfully inviting, not mushy.

Beat in the olive oil, lemon juice and seasonings, and chill at least two hours. I recommend being conservative with both the oil and lemon; you can always add more as the flavors have a chance to blend. To serve, place several large, toasty garlic croutons in each bowl and pour soup around. For that special touch, serve this Spanish salad-soup in chilled bowls with icy-cold soup spoons.

SERVES 12.

TOMATOES STUFFED WITH DEVILED EGGS

A popular appetizer that can be done with cherry or regular tomatoes.

INGREDIENTS

24 cherry tomatoes or
6 medium ripe tomatoes
•
10 hardboiled eggs, shelled and
chopped
•
1 cup chopped celery
•
1/4 cup chopped onion (can be white
and green mixed)
•
2 tablespoons chopped green pepper
•
1/4 cup mayonnaise
•
3 teaspoons mustard
•
1 teaspoon salt, or to taste
•
1/8 teaspoon cayenne or lemon
pepper
•
Vinegar and lemon juice to taste
•
French dressing

After removing stem end, quarter regular tomatoes from top almost to bottom, pressing sections out. Sprinkle with salt, pepper and bottled French dressing. Prepare deviled egg mixture and fill tomato quarters. For cherry tomatoes, cut off stem end, squeeze seeds out, drain and fill. To vary, try this with Balsamic vinegar.

MAKES 24 APPETIZERS.

DRIED TOMATOES

Roma or plum tomatoes are used for drying. If you don't have a dehydrator, no problem – the oven does it just fine. *Sunset Magazine* gave instructions some years ago for drying tomatoes in the oven, and that's the way I do it. You simply cut them open, sprinkle the small halves lightly with salt, and place (cut side up) on a rack in a shallow pan or cookie sheet. Bake at 200 degrees until they feel dry, but not brittle, and are shriveled and flat. This process takes 7 to 9 hours. Five pounds of tomatoes will make about ten ounces of dried tomatoes. They can be eaten dried, stored loosely in a jar for

adding to sauces, or packed in olive oil for numerous recipes. Recently I've noted many of the trendy gourmet pizza shops use rehydrated tomatoes as a topping.

I used to buy the intensely flavored dried romas in Seattle on my way back to Anchorage. Once I learned how to dry them myself, however, it was a simple step to pack them in olive oil. Again, *Sunset* provided the directions.

DRIED TOMATOES IN OLIVE OIL

INGREDIENTS

3 pounds dried roma tomatoes

•

2 teaspoons salt

•

2 six-inch sprigs of rosemary, or
1 tablespoon dry leaves

•

About 1-1/4 cups olive oil

Cover tomatoes completely with oil and put in jar with lid. They will keep at room temperature as long as the olive oil tastes fresh. For longer storage, refrigerate.

SWEET AND SOUR TOMATO SALAD

INGREDIENTS

4 large ripe tomatoes, sliced

•

1 large white onion, sliced paper thin

•

1 cucumber, partially peeled, sliced

•

1/2 green bell pepper, sliced crosswise

•

Vinegar and water to cover

•

Sugar or equal to taste

•

Salt, pepper and Mrs. Dash

Place all ingredients in non-corrosive dish and refrigerate. Keeps several days. Add more vegetables to the vinegar-water solution as they are eaten. Experiment with wine, balsamic, or herb-flavored vinegar to find your favorite. A very popular, refreshing salad, and hardly a calorie in it.

SERVES 6-8.

YAMS AND SWEET POTATOES

The ten-pound bags of yams or sweet potatoes at the warehouse are a good food and nutrition investment. They should have smooth, even-colored skin with few blemishes, although blemishes don't necessarily indicate a bad potato. Both yams (the more orange-colored potato) and sweet potatoes (the paler version) keep a long time in a cool, dry place. They also do well tied individually in panty hose (see onion storage). Don't refrigerate as neither potato likes cold temperatures. However, once cooked, they freeze just fine sliced and packaged in airtight zipper bags. Warm them in the microwave in the same bag on medium power, then season.

Yams or sweet potatoes are a delightful change from the usual starchy vegetable served at home but, too often, we forget they're around. The small ones are convenient for baking and serving individually, with the larger ones destined for casseroles, etc. Although seldom served plain and simple, there is absolutely nothing wrong with butter, salt and pepper for seasoning these tasty boiled, baked or fried potatoes. To intensify their flavor when baking, leave them in the oven until they cool down to room temperature.

Yams and sweet potatoes also go well with pineapple, citrus and dried fruits, so experiment with various combinations.

LOUISIANA CANDIED YAMS OR SWEET POTATOES

INGREDIENTS

3 pounds potatoes
•
1 1/2 cups dark brown sugar
•
5 tablespoons butter or margarine
•
2 1/2 cups water
•
1 teaspoon grated orange peel
•
1 1/2 teaspoons cinnamon
•
1 1/2 teaspoons vanilla
•
3 tablespoons rum (optional)

My Cajun friends looked with disdain at anyone who would merely sprinkle seasonings over candied yams. No, it must be done this way. First you put the whole, unpeeled potatoes in a large pot of water. Cook with water slowly boiling for an hour or until done. Drain, cool and peel the potatoes. Meanwhile, make a syrup from the remaining ingredients (except rum) in a saucepan. Simmer the syrup about half an hour; it will reduce and thicken slightly.

Lay the peeled potato slices in a buttered casserole dish. Sprinkle with salt and rum. Pour the syrup over the potato slices, coating thoroughly. Bake at 450 degrees, basting every 10 minutes until syrup is bubbly and potatoes have taken on a caramel color, about 30-40 minutes. Let cool in syrup, which absorbs and thickens as it cools. Reheat in microwave.

SERVES 10-12.

JAMMIN' YAMS

An unusual but captivating way to serve yams. Get the work and mess out of the way early.
Bake the casserole the next day or for tonight's dinner.

INGREDIENTS

4 cups yams, cooked

•

1/4 cup butter

•

3/4 cup onion, chopped

•

1/4 cup flour

•

1/4 teaspoon dry mustard

•

1/2 teaspoon *each* salt, pepper and
dried basil

•

1 1/2 cups milk

•

1 1/2 cups grated Swiss cheese

•

2 cups baked ham, diced

Cook unpeeled yams in boiling water until tender. When cool, peel and cut into quarter-inch slices. In skillet, melt butter and sauté onions. Stir in flour, mustard, salt, pepper and basil; simmer to blend. Add milk and bring to a boil, stirring constantly until thickened. Remove from heat and stir in half the grated cheese and all the ham.

Rub a large casserole with butter and pour half of the sauce over the bottom. Cover with a layer of yam slices, another layer of sauce, and finish with yams on top. Refrigerate or bake (30 minutes at 325 degrees), then cover casserole with remaining Swiss cheese. Return to oven several minutes until cheese is melted.

SERVES 6-8.

SWEET POTATO SPICE CAKE

I've tried several versions of sweet potato cakes and finally settled on this one. The recipe came from a bakery in Detroit known as Sweet Potato Sensations, so I figured the owner, Cassandra Thomas, must be the expert.

INGREDIENTS

2 1/2 cups flour

2 teaspoons *each* baking soda and baking powder

1/4 teaspoon salt

2 teaspoons *each* cinnamon and nutmeg

1 cup *each* brown and granulated sugar

1 1/2 cups margarine

3 large eggs

1 tablespoon vanilla

2 1/2 cups mashed sweet potatoes

1/2 cup crushed pineapple, drained

1 cup *each* raisins and chopped walnuts

Preheat oven to 350 degrees. Grease and flour two 9-inch cake pans or three 8-inch pans. Mix the flour, baking soda and powder, salt, spices and sugars in a large bowl. Add one egg, margarine and vanilla and blend with electric mixer on low speed, then on medium for two minutes.

Scrape down sides and add eggs, one at a time, beating well after each. Add sweet potatoes, pineapple, raisins and walnuts. Blend on low until thoroughly mixed. Spread into cake pans. Bake 60 to 70 minutes. A toothpick inserted in center should come out clean. Cool in pans 10 minutes, then invert on rack and cool.

FROSTING:

In medium bowl, beat 2 cups cream cheese and 1/3 cup butter until smooth. Add 1 tablespoon vanilla and mix well. Gradually add 3 cups powdered sugar and beat on low speed until smooth. Optional: Add 1 teaspoon rum flavoring. Spread on cake.

BEANS, PASTA AND RICE

INTRODUCTION

If you have a supply of pasta, rice and precooked beans on hand, there are endless choices for creating mouth-watering dishes in the shortest of time. Beans are high in protein and fiber content and, when served with rice, nuts or dairy products, become complete proteins, that provide essential amino acids. Pasta and rice also lend themselves to combinations resulting in complete proteins. Nutritional meatless diets are easy to achieve with these essential staples.

More than half the world's population thrives on a diet of rice with bits of this and that thrown in, and they live longer, healthier lives than Americans. Complex carbohydrate foods such as rice, pasta, legumes, bread, grains, fruits and vegetables are great energy sources – high in fiber and low in fat. They also are filling.

Give me some beans, pasta or rice, some chicken broth, onions and peppers, and I'll cook up something good. Try it yourself. Start with rice and no recipe – just look in the refrigerator, freezer or pantry and imagine what might go well with it. "Ingredient cooking" relies heavily on these foods and, besides being good for us, they're inexpensive. At the warehouses, you can buy pinto beans as inexpensively as 40 cents a pound, long-grain rice for about 25 cents a pound, and pasta for just over 60 cents a pound.

—BEANS—

Purchase different varieties of dried beans in bulk and store them in airtight containers such as canning jars. We sometimes forget that dried beans don't keep forever. If they are too old, they will remain hard no matter how long you cook them. Be sure to compare the cost of 3-, 5- or 10-pound bags of dried beans with the sizes you normally buy to see how much money you can save.

Precooked frozen beans can help save the day when combined with many other ingredients covered on these pages. My favorites are black turtle beans, pintos, kidney beans, navy beans and limas. A quick thaw in the microwave, and you'll have the basic ingredient for baked beans, soups, refries, dips, salsas, salads and casseroles. And from a nutritional standpoint, just one cup of cooked beans contains half the recommended daily amount of fiber.

Beans for your ingredient storehouse: Say you plan to spend Saturday morning on some kitchen projects. That's a good time for simmering two or three varieties of beans. Soak beans the night before and simmer them very slowly while you keep an eye on them. Refrigerate or freeze in jars, zipper bags, or plastic containers until ready to use. As opposed to the preseasoned canned varieties, you can season dried beans the way you like. Just note on the labels any special seasonings you've added. Use them in these recipes or develop your own.

MEXICAN LAYERED APPETIZER

There are numerous versions of this popular and tasty appetizer; it's a great take-along dish. With your ingredients on hand, you can put it together in a flash.

INGREDIENTS

1/2 head lettuce, shredded

•

2 cups cooked pinto beans, mashed

•

1/4 cup taco sauce

•

2 cups avocado, mashed

•

2 cups sour cream, or sour cream substitute

•

2 cups cheddar cheese, grated

•

Green onions, sliced

•

Black olives, sliced

•

2 tomatoes, chopped, seeded and drained

Mix red taco sauce with mashed pinto beans and set aside. Cover the bottom of a large, rimmed serving dish with crisp shredded lettuce. Spread the beans over the lettuce. For the next layer, spread the avocado. Cover with real or imitation sour cream. Top with grated cheddar cheese. Arrange over the top of the dish circles of green onions, black olives and tomatoes. Serve with tortilla chips. If you prefer making this early in the day, hold the chopped tomatoes until ready to serve.

Precise measurements or order are not important for this recipe. You can vary it by adding ground beef or shredded pork, corn, Monterey jack cheese or other salsas on top. Take care, however, that all the ingredients are well-drained.

SERVES 10 TO 15 AS AN APPETIZER.

CALDO GALLEGO

This spectacular bean soup has been served at many a large winter party. I cook (and serve) it in a 3-gallon enamel-clad pot, right off the stove. This is no ordinary bean soup, as you will see when everyone goes back for more. The combination of beans, sausages, ham, potatoes and spinach is hearty and attractive. Have copies of the recipe handy, as guests always want it.

INGREDIENTS

3 or 4 cups small white navy beans

•

One or two large ham hocks

•

2 cups chopped onion

•

4 cups water

•

2 quarts chicken broth

•

Chopped green bell pepper and
jalapeño pepper, optional

•

1 pound breakfast link sausages

•

1 pound Louisiana hot links

•

2 or 3 Idaho potatoes

•

1 pound fresh or frozen spinach

Soak beans overnight in a large bowl covered with water. Separately, place ham hocks and onions in a heavy, large pot. Add enough water to cover and let pot simmer several hours or overnight. (You can eliminate this cooking step, but I think it gives the soup more character.)

Next morning, mix chicken base in two quarts water (or broth from cooking a chicken) and add this to the onion-ham broth. Cut the meat from the well-done ham hocks and put meat back in pot. Drain the soaking water from the navy beans, and add them to the pot. Toss in a little chopped green bell pepper and chopped jalapeño if you like.

Simmer the beans very slowly for an hour or two, partially covered. In a skillet, brown the breakfast sausages and Louisiana hot links until crispy. Slice the cooled link sausages in half and the hot links into bite-size pieces. Drain both on paper towels before adding to soup pot. Cut potatoes in large dice and add to soup, cooking until potatoes are done. If soup looks watery, remove some of the beans, whirl in blender and return to the pot. All this can be done a day ahead, which I usually do to allow the flavors to blend.

To prepare for serving, slowly reheat the soup on the stove or in the oven. Add the loosely chopped spinach and reheat. (This is a great way to use the triple-washed spinach from those large warehouse bags.) Serve in heated bowls if convenient. Reheat smaller quantities in the microwave, and freeze any leftover soup in bags or jars.

Warning: Thick soups like this one scorch easily – I speak from experience. If such a mishap occurs, transfer the soup to other containers without scraping the burned part from the bottom of the pot. I have better luck reheating large quantities of bean soups in the oven at no higher than 300 degrees.

SERVES UP TO 25.

BLACK BEAN AND PEPPER SALAD

This jewel of a salad recipe which appeared in the Los Angeles Times in 1988, serves a crowd. With these ingredients, it is colorful and spicy. Prepare a day or so ahead to let flavors blend and let you relax before the party.

INGREDIENTS

2 pounds dried black beans
•
1 large bay leaf
•
1 1/2 tablespoons cumin seeds
•
1/2 cup sherry wine vinegar
•
2/3 cup extra-virgin olive oil
•
1 large white onion, finely diced
•
2 medium green, 1 red and one yellow
bell pepper, all finely diced
•
2 jalapeño chiles, seeded and minced
•
2 garlic cloves, pressed through
mill or minced
•
1 1/2 teaspoons salt
•
Freshly ground pepper

Rinse beans and check for stones or dirt. Cover with cold water and soak overnight. Pour beans into colander and rinse again, then place in large pot with bay leaf and fresh water to cover by two inches. Bring to boil, reduce heat and simmer until tender but firm, 1 1/2 to 2 hours. Drain beans and discard bay leaf.

Toast cumin seeds in skillet over moderately high heat, stirring until seeds are toasted and fragrant, about 2 minutes. Set aside. In large bowl combine warm beans with vinegar and oil. Add onion, peppers, jalapeños, garlic, cumin seeds. Toss and let stand, mixing occasionally, as salad cools. Add freshly ground pepper to taste. Cover and refrigerate.

SERVES 16-20.

FEFI'S CUBAN BLACK BEANS AND RICE

This is the way I remember my cousin Fefi preparing black beans; it's also the Cuban national dish, one that I fell in love with when I tasted it in Havana. Black beans are full of flavor, as you will see when you try them. For a dinner party, serve as a soup course without the rice, or as an entrée with rice and condiments. Bread, salad, coffee with anisette liqueur and a light dessert fill out the menu.

INGREDIENTS

1 pound black beans
•
1 white onion, quartered
•
1 green pepper, quartered
•
2 cloves garlic
•
1 bay leaf

Rinse, sort and soak beans overnight in water with other four ingredients. Next day, drain the liquid off and put the beans and seasonings in a pot and cover with chicken broth or water. Cook slowly two or three hours, adding more liquid as needed. Freeze for future use or proceed to next step.

→

MORE INGREDIENTS

1 white onion, diced
•
1 green pepper, diced
•
1/2 to 1 tablespoon olive oil
•
Cumin
•
Cayenne pepper
•
Salt
•
3 tablespoons sherry
•
Lemon slices
•
Cooked rice

An hour or so before serving, fry another onion and green pepper, chopped, in olive oil. Add to beans and simmer together. At this point I usually remove half of the soup, blend it and return it to the pot. Season conservatively with ground cumin, cayenne pepper and salt. A few minutes before serving, put a couple of lemon slices in the pot and add 3 tablespoons of sherry.

Cook white rice separately and put a mound in each heated soup plate. Pour the soup around and garnish with lemon slice, chopped egg yolks and green onions.

SERVES 8 AS A MAIN COURSE.

SPICY BARBECUE SAUCE

INGREDIENTS

15-ounce can tomato sauce
•
6 ounces tomato paste
•
1 1/2 cups V-8 juice or Snappy Tom Mix
•
1/4 cup vinegar
•
3 tablespoons Worcestershire sauce
•
3 tablespoons butter
•
1 cup brown sugar
•
1/2 teaspoon *each* cayenne, nutmeg, cinnamon and allspice
•
1 teaspoon *each* black pepper, Tabasco, mustard, garlic powder and paprika
•
2 teaspoons chili powder, Cajun seasoning or barbecue spice
•
2 tablespoons molasses

Put ingredients in saucepan and simmer for 45 minutes. If too thick, add water. Pour sauce over beans or use on chicken, beef or pork ribs.

ANN'S CRAZY MIXED-UP BAKED BEANS (FOR THE GANG)

My friend Ann Parrish, one of the <u>Electric Bread</u> cookbook creators, first served this fabulous conglomeration to members of our women's group. Each summer we spend a weekend at the Parrish cabin on Big Lake, an event we call the "Low-Costa Spa." (We order products from the La Costa Spa and pretend we're actually there. Truth be known, we probably have more fun!)

INGREDIENTS

2 cups onion, chopped
•
1 cup celery, chopped
•
1 or 2 jalapeños, chopped
•
2 cups peppers (red, green, yellow)
•
4 slices bacon
•
6 Italian sausages
•
Barbecue sauce (Bullseye)

Sauté onion in non-stick skillet. Add celery, jalapeños and bell peppers and simmer until soft. In a large pot fry bacon and Italian sausages, crumbled. Drain off excess grease and combine meat and sautéed vegetables. Add seven 16-ounce cans of beans, each different, drained in colander. Select from your freezer supply or from cans:

Pinto beans
Large red kidney beans
Pork and beans
Yellow wax beans
Cut green beans
Black-eyed peas
Garbanzo beans
Navy or lima beans
Chili beans
Black beans

Mix all this together and cover with barbecue sauce. Bake at 325 degrees for an hour. *NOTE:* Measurements and ingredients may be substituted with abandon in this recipe!

SERVES 20.

KATHRYN'S BLACK BEAN DIP WITH SALSA

This dip is a regular at family functions. My daughter makes it a day ahead and refrigerates until ready to serve.

INGREDIENTS

3 cups black beans, cooked

•

2 cloves garlic, minced

•

1/2 teaspoon *each* salt, cayenne pepper and cumin

SALSA:

1/3 cup hot peppers (jalapeño, Fresnos, serranos or combination)

•

1/4 cup cilantro, finely chopped

•

Juice of 2 limes (1/3 cup)

•

1 cup sour cream

Place beans, garlic and seasonings in blender and blend until smooth. Spread beans over bottom of serving dish that allows dip to be about 1/2 inch deep. Seed and finely chop peppers and combine with cilantro and lime juice. Mix well. Spread over beans. Before serving, place dollops of sour cream or sour cream substitute onto the bean mixture in whatever artful design inspires you. Serve with your favorite tortilla chips.

— P A S T A —

Remember, years ago, when elbow macaroni, two sizes of spaghetti, and egg noodles were about all the pasta we used? Not today, with pasta such a popular food; there are hundreds of varieties and sizes. With the great selection of pasta now being carried by the warehouse stores, I find it more and more difficult to justify lugging out my electric pasta machine. Homemade pasta is always a special treat (and good therapy), but it is time-consuming to make.

The best pasta is made from semolina flour, also called durum. You can buy the warehouse-size packages of dried pasta knowing they will last indefinitely with proper storage. Protect your purchase from heat and sunlight, and store dried pasta in airtight containers. The lemon pepper and basil garlic linguini are a couple of my favorites.

I've been pleasantly surprised with the warehouse selection of fresh ravioli, tortellini, and seasoned dry pasta varieties. It is so easy to add one of your frozen sauces to any of these excellent products. Or, simply heat the cooked pasta in a little extra-virgin olive oil and toss with freshly grated parmesan or romano and a few herbs. Fresh pasta keeps several days wrapped airtight in the refrigerator, longer if unopened, and it will keep for months in the freezer. Lasagne and cannelloni keep particularly well for long periods.

When you've cooked too much pasta, immediately wrap and refrigerate the excess – hot pasta tonight can be pasta salad in a day or two. There's no federal law that says pasta must be cooked just before serving. When you're cooking for company, it's nice not to have to deal with steaming pots of water, and draining and saucing pasta at the last minute.

The solution? Cook the pasta at a more convenient time, even two or three days before the meal. (No one will notice the difference.) Rinse with icy water to stop the cooking, drain, toss with a light oil or butter and "bag" it when cool. Use "as is" for salads, or heat it right in the zipper bag in the microwave oven (on medium power), fresh from the refrigerator.

For some reason, pasta seems to cool quicker than other foods meant to be served hot. It is a real challenge to keep it the right temperature until everyone is served. Heated plates and serving dishes are a must. Whenever possible, combine the pasta and sauce in a heated skillet before serving.

LEMON-PEPPER PASTA WITH SHRIMP

My sister Diane served this pasta at her hotel in Bethel, Alaska, and it was a hit.
If you have it, use penne rigate or linguini pasta already seasoned with lemon and pepper.

INGREDIENTS

4 cups cooked and drained lemon-
pepper pasta

•

1 pound shrimp, unshelled

•

1/2 tablespoon olive oil

•

3 green onions, sliced

•

3 garlic cloves, minced

•

1 tablespoon flour

•

1/4 teaspoon *each* salt, pepper, nutmeg
and paprika

•

3/4 cup shrimp broth and
3/4 cup chicken broth

•

1/4 cup milk

•

2 tablespoons tomato paste

Peel and devein shrimp, reserving shells. Cover just the shells with 2 cups water and bring to a boil. Reduce heat and simmer until stock is reduced to 3/4 cup. Strain the shells and set stock aside. Heat olive oil in skillet and sauté onions and garlic in the oil. Add flour and seasonings, cooking a minute or so.

To the skillet add the shrimp and chicken broth, stirring until mixture thickens. Add milk, tomato paste and shrimp, simmering just until shrimp is no longer translucent, about five minutes. Thin with water or white wine if necessary. Toss with hot pasta and serve on heated plates.

SERVES 4.

FAIRSEA SPAGHETTI

You may never try this recipe, but it was served at the captain's table on the Fairsea cruise ship years ago, on its Alaska Inside Passage cruise. I was impressed with the pasta *and* the captain, as I recall.

Serve this right out of the skillet. Sauté finely shredded prosciutto in unsalted butter. Mix with capellini pasta. Add warm whipping cream and, with a grand flourish, toss the pasta with sevruga caviar at a zillion dollars an ounce and serve immediately with $75 champagne in icy-cold flutes.

PASTA PRIMAVERA

This is a fancy name for whatever is in the refrigerator or freezer that would be good on pasta – in a hurry. By using what you have on hand, it tastes different every time. The secret is to keep some crunch in the vegetables.

INGREDIENTS

Penne or mostaccioli,
1 pound dried, cooked

•

3 tablespoons mild olive oil

•

1 large garlic clove, minced

•

5 shallots, or 5 green onions, minced

•

2 cups fresh tomatoes, diced

•

1 cup broccoli flowerets

•

1/2 red bell pepper, sliced

•

1 cup snow peas

•

1/2 cup miniature pickled corn,
halved

•

10 miniature zucchini, whole, or 1 cup
regular zucchini, diced

•

6 large mushrooms, sliced

•

1/4 cup chopped fresh basil and/or
Italian parsley

•

Salt and freshly ground pepper

•

Freshly-grated parmesan or
romano cheese

Have a pot of boiling water on the stove. In a colander or large strainer, lower and hold the broccoli, peas, peppers and zucchini in the water for about three minutes or until barely tender. Remove and rinse with cold water. Set aside. Reheat pasta in microwave or in a colander over boiling water.

Sauté garlic, shallots, herbs and tomatoes in olive oil. Add vegetables and heat through. Toss with hot pasta and serve with grated cheese.

SERVES 6-8.

AWARD-WINNING SHRIMP AND PASTA SALAD

A woman named Sandy Boling entered this recipe in the Brinnon, Washington, Shrimpfest recently, and it took first prize.

INGREDIENTS

12 ounces rotelle pasta, cooked and drained

•

1 pound cooked, shelled shrimp

•

2 large tomatoes, diced

•

1 cup baby carrots, thinly sliced

•

1 each green and red bell pepper, diced

•

1 purple onion, diced

•

1/2 cup (about) ripe olives, sliced

•

1 16-ounce bottle Kraft Zesty Italian dressing

•

1 cup each cauliflower and broccoli flowerets

•

1/4 cup parmesan cheese

•

1 tablespoon sesame seed

•

2 teaspoons poppy seed

•

1 teaspoon paprika

•

1/2 teaspoon celery seed

•

1/4 teaspoon garlic powder

•

1 cup yellow summer squash, optional

•

1/2 cup mushrooms, quartered, optional

Combine all ingredients in a covered container and refrigerate overnight.

SERVES 10 TO 15.

— RICE —

Warehouse packages of the best rice on the market are available from grande to humongous (50-pound bags), so take your pick. You can also find seasoned rice blends and excellent combinations of rice with freeze-dried vegetables. Once opened, the rice must be stored airtight in a cool place. Used plastic buckets from the corner restaurant or bakery are great and usually free, so make friends with the kitchen staff.

White rice keeps a year or more, brown up to six months. To keep it even longer – no, I haven't gone over the edge – refrigerate or freeze your rice. In summertime Alamos, where temperatures skyrocket and bugs abound, freezing rice is not unusual.

I have had some notable disasters with rice-cooking, so this section shares lessons I've learned the hard way. Gummy rice, scorched rice, soupy rice, hard-as-a-rock rice; I've done them all, and not just once. The worst was a fancy dinner party featuring Paella Valenciana, complete with budget-breaking lobster, shrimp, pork, chicken, chorizo and clams. What could the guests say as they crunched down on uncooked rice? Little did I know the rice was simply too old.

Lesson 1. The older the rice, the more liquid and time needed to cook it.

Lesson 2. Brown rice takes much longer to cook than long-grain white.

Lesson 3. Don't open the rice pot or the steam will escape; steam cooks the rice.

Lesson 4. Cook the rice ahead; then microwave in zipper bags to heat.

Lesson 5. When all else fails, use a rice cooker.

Charmaine Solomon's *Complete Vegetarian Cookbook*, a stunning collection of international recipes anyone would enjoy, has some great rice-cooking recommendations. Solomon's book is the first I've noted that thoroughly clarifies the needs of different rice varieties and proportions.

She recommends the absorption cooking method. This involves carefully measuring the water and rice, and cooking it in a pot with tight-fitting lid. The water and rice go in together, and as soon as the water boils, the lid goes on and timing starts. Note these differences in timing:

White long-grain rice: 2 cups water for 1 cup rice; 1 1/2 cups water for each additional cup of rice. Cooking time after reaching boiling point: 18-20 minutes, simmered on very low heat.

White short or medium-grain rice: 1 1/2 cups water for 1 cup rice; 1 cup water for each additional cup of rice. Cooking time after reaching boiling point: 12-15 minutes, simmered on very low heat.

Natural, brown or unpolished rice: Use same proportions as for long-grain white rice, but cook 35 minutes longer.

There are virtually unlimited uses for cooked rice, and recipe books are replete with excellent ideas for incorporating rice into meals several times a week. Rice can also be easily substituted for pasta, polenta, couscous or other grains in many recipes – just use your imagination.

PAELLA VALENCIANA

This is the version I ruined on the first try. Before cooking paella, have all ingredients cleaned, chopped and ready.
Your challenge will be to find a skillet large enough if you don't have a paella pan.
(I bought a deep slope-sided non-stick skillet at Costco, and it works very well for this dish.)
If you're not sure your skillet is big enough, estimate the volume of all the ingredients and measure cups of water in the skillet.
If necessary, divide ingredients (after cooking the rice) between two skillets.

INGREDIENTS

Cook together:

1/2 to 1 cup olive oil

1 pound chorizo, crumbled

1 large green pepper, chopped

1 medium red onion, chopped

4 cloves garlic, minced

1 teaspoon crushed red pepper

Stir in:

2 1/2 cups long-grain white rice

3 cups clam juice

1 cup white wine

10 pieces saffron or to taste

Salt and pepper

1 tablespoon fresh basil

1 1/2 cups artichoke hearts,
from can or freezer

After sautéing the first six ingredients, add the next seven ingredients and bring to boil, stirring. Cover pan with lid or foil and bake in a 350-degree oven for 30 minutes. Fluff the rice and set aside.

Add to hot rice:

1 1/2 pounds white fish fillets, cut in 1-inch pieces

1 dozen or more raw clams in shell, scrubbed

1 pound medium raw shrimp, shelled and deveined

1 pound raw mussels in shell, scrubbed and debearded

2 ripe tomatoes, seeded and chopped

1 cup green beans, fresh or frozen (thawed)

1/2 cup peas, fresh or frozen (thawed)

1 teaspoon paprika

2 pounds king or snow crab legs (hold for top)

Heat until shells open and fish is done. Keep warm. Arrange crab legs on top and return to oven to reheat to serving temperature. Garnish with lemon slices and parsley and serve the paella from the pan.

SERVES 20-25.

SUN'S UP RICE PUDDING

This quick and easy breakfast or dessert pudding uses instant rice. Combine in a saucepan or microwave dish:

INGREDIENTS

1 cup uncooked instant rice
•
1 1/2 cups milk
•
3 tablespoons honey
•
1/2 teaspoon salt
•
1/2 teaspoon cinnamon or nutmeg
•
1/2 cup raisins and 1/2 cut dried apples or apricots.

Bring to a full boil, stirring. Remove from heat and, with lid on tight, let the rice stand for 15 minutes. Serve with milk or cream. You can also combine the ingredients the night before and refrigerate. Because the liquids will absorb overnight, the pudding is practically ready to serve; just heat in the microwave.

SERVES 4-6.

FOLLOWING ARE TWO EXCELLENT CURRIED RICE SALADS THAT YOU CAN COUNT ON BEING A HIT AT YOUR HOUSE OR AT A POTLUCK BUFFET.

FRUITY BROWN RICE SALAD

INGREDIENTS

4 cups brown rice, cooked
•
1 cup raw carrot, chopped
•
One 11-ounce can mandarin oranges, drained
•
1 apple, diced
•
1 cup pineapple chunks, fresh, frozen or canned
•
1 cup seedless red or green grapes, halved
•
1/2 cup *each* raisins, toasted pine nuts and chopped walnuts
•
1/2 cup *each* whipping cream and mayonnaise (or yogurt)
•
2 tablespoons chutney, chopped
•
1 tablespoon *each* curry powder and lemon juice
•
Salt and freshly ground pepper to taste

Mix ingredients well. Chill.

SERVES 10-12 AS A SIDE DISH.

DIANE'S CURRIED RICE SALAD

My sister pulled this recipe together for a conference of high school officials at her hotel; the fishing boat that was to have brought in fresh king salmon didn't show. It took a few phone calls to friends to find fresh bananas, but that's the way it's done in the bush. She offered to adjust the bill, but the salad was such a hit the conference coordinator declined – on one condition: that Diane share the recipe. The quantities listed here will feed a dozen or so.

INGREDIENTS

4 cups chicken breast, poached
and diced
•
1 red bell pepper, diced
•
3/4 cup pickled cocktail onions
•
1/2 cup *each* raisins and currants
•
4 cups white rice, cooked
•
1/2 cup dried apricots, chopped
•
1 cup fresh pineapple in 1" chunks
•
1/2 cup pine nuts
•
2 cups bananas, sliced
•
1/4 cup parsley, minced
•
5 tablespoons dark rum

Soften raisins and currants in rum.
Mix them with other ingredients.

Toss salad with dressing prepared as follows:

INGREDIENTS

•
2 tablespoons fresh or frozen lime juice
•
1 egg (lightly beaten)
•
1 teaspoon dry mustard
•
1/4 teaspoon *each* salt and pepper
•
1/2 teaspoon garlic powder
•
1 1/4 cups vegetable oil
•
1/2 cup sour cream
•
1 1/2 tablespoons curry powder
•

Garnish: Hard-boiled eggs, cherry tomatoes or pepper rings

Mix lime juice, egg, dry mustard, and seasonings (except curry powder) in a blender or food processor. With motor running, gradually add vegetable oil, blending until mixture thickens. Add sour cream and curry powder. Adjust seasonings as needed.

Serve rice on a large platter or in a shallow bowl surrounded by sliced hard-boiled eggs, cherry tomatoes, or pepper rings.

SERVES 12-14.

HOMEMADE INGREDIENTS

INTRODUCTION

Your new style of cooking, which allows you to quickly create well-balanced meals from partially prepared ingredients, will benefit by having the recipe components in this section on hand. Cooking them from scratch can be messy and take time and effort to accomplish, but if you prepare larger quantities with future uses in mind, you are well ahead of the game. I tend to undertake such projects when I'm in the kitchen anyway. My theory is, why not make better use of the time?

Some cooks shy away from making sauces and gravies, thinking there's some sort of elusive skill involved. Not true. If you can stir, you can do either. It's not like you're required to do it the way we did in the "olden days." At our lodge in the early '60s, for instance, the way we made a rich, dark brown meat stock was to fill a huge pressure cooker with moose and caribou bones, leftover beef, vegetables and spices for seasoning, and simmer it in water on the wood stove for two or three days. Thank goodness, today, someone else does the hard part for us.

— BEEF BROTH —

Either Tone's or Knorr's Gourmet Edge beef flavoring base, available in 1-pound jars at Sam's or Costco, is essential for your ingredient arsenal. Throw away the bouillon cubes; these products are superior and more convenient. Use in soups, gravy, stews, chili and casseroles for that slow-cooked, homemade flavor. Refrigerate after opening.

— BEEF DRIPPINGS —

There are times when you demand rich, pure beef drippings, and only the real thing will do. One of those times is when roast beef and Yorkshire pudding are on the menu. The solution to the age-old problem of how to avoid last-minute sauce and gravy making came to me during the GREAT YORKSHIRE PUDDING CRISIS. A lodge kitchen staffer had quickly washed the roasting pan *before* the succulent prime rib drippings could be poured off and measured for the Yorkshire pudding. There would be none of the long-coveted pudding. I shrieked. I fainted. When I came to, I vowed never again to allow such a crisis to occur.

The Solution: Surreptitiously acquire the pan juices ahead of time, which I now do. How? Make friends with your neighborhood restaurateur and ask the chef to save you a quart of beef drippings. Since many restaurants prepare rare roast beef regularly, the chef will surely comply with your request. The drippings can be frozen until you need them.

Today, when my guests are served a "last-minute" sauce, Yorkshire pudding or roast beef gravy, it miraculously appears in heated carafes – no muss, no fuss. Since we're on the subject of Yorkshire pudding, here is the easy recipe:

YORKSHIRE PUDDING FOR 16

INGREDIENTS

Beef drippings
•
3 cups milk
•
3 cups flour
•
6 eggs, beaten
•
1-1/2 teaspoons salt
•
Freshly ground pepper

Well before serving time, arrange two non-stick muffin tins (for large muffins) on a counter. In each section, ladle up to a tablespoon of beef drippings; set tins aside – you don't fill them yet.

For the pudding, add the milk and flour alternately to the beaten eggs, stirring. Add 3 tablespoons of beef drippings to the batter, mix well, and season with salt and pepper. Pour all into a half-gallon pitcher for later use.

When the roast is done, raise the oven temperature to 450 degrees. Slide the muffin tins in to preheat the drippings, if desired, for a firmer crust. About 20 minutes prior to serving the meat course, fill each muffin section half full of batter and return to oven. Set a timer for 20 minutes; check the pudding; if it is fully puffed and firm, it is done. Otherwise reduce heat to 350 degrees for another 10 minutes. Release each muffin with a knife and pass while the meat course is being served. Note: The pudding can also be poured into square pans or Pyrex dishes. For non-stick surfaces, lightly butter any area the pudding touches so it releases easier.

—CHICKEN BROTH—

Buy the 1-pound jars of moist chicken soup base from the warehouse (Tone's or Knorr's Gourmet Edge) instead of using expensive canned chicken broth. It's good, you can prepare the precise amount you need, and the base keeps indefinitely in the refrigerator. While a teaspoon mixed with water makes a cup of broth, the undiluted base can go into any number of dishes for that rich chicken flavor.

CHICKEN BROTH, HOMEMADE

Don't even think about tossing the carcass and skin removed from roasted chicken. Simmer it with water in a pot, add salt, a carrot, some celery, parsley and onion, and you have extra chicken broth to freeze or use for soup or chicken pot pie. Better still, make some chicken broth from uncooked chicken. You might have some of the warehouse chicken parts that have been around too long – toss them in the stock pot.

You don't need the best parts of the chicken to make good broth. I learned this years ago when I was an expert at being poor. My girlfriend's parents owned a famous Anchorage establishment, The Lucky Wishbone. Her family and mine were the fortunate recipients of large bags of chicken backs, necks and wings not needed at the restaurant. We prepared these orphaned parts every way imaginable and, to this day, I can't see a chicken neck without remembering that period of life – which wasn't all that intolerable in retrospect.

To make your own hearty chicken broth, put raw and/or cooked chicken parts in a large pot, and cover with water. Add 2 large diced onions, 4 cups of carrots and 4 cups of celery, diced, a bay leaf, a half cup of chopped parsley, salt, pepper and some Mrs. Dash seasoning. Throw in a few giblets if you have them.

Cover the pot and simmer the broth for two or three hours. Chill the broth and remove the congealed fat layer from the top. Just a few minutes of your time and some inexpensive ingredients give you a nice supply of rich, purely delicious chicken broth.

You will also have a flavorful cache of meat from the bones, which can be frozen and used for other purposes. Serve it in tortillas with fresh vegetables and salsa. Use some for chicken salad or for flavoring soups and casseroles. Almost any vegetable puree that you have frozen blends perfectly with chicken broth for a tasty hot soup.

— GRAVY (ROUX) —

Sinfully rich, mouth-watering gravy. Southern cooks can do it, so why can't everyone? If you've ever had biscuits and wallpaper paste, you can bet a southerner was not manning the skillet. The secret is the browning process. Even with light gravies, the flour must be browned enough to remove the raw flour taste.

Approximately equal parts of flour and either butter, bacon grease, olive oil, or fat skimmed from cooked meat are slowly browned before adding liquid. Not only does the patient browning make the gravy taste superb, it will look like gravy is supposed to look.

My grandmother taught me how to make gravy (the kind that makes you eat more mashed potatoes just so you'll have something to put it on), and basic cookbooks contain good directions. This section, however, is about making a roux, and the lesson came not from grandma, but from Cajun friends who came to Alaska from Crowley, Louisiana. It is the base for many Cajun dishes.

The rule, Ron and Wanda LaFleur taught me, is to brown the flour and fat over low heat, very slowly. How slowly? Forty-five minutes slowly, that's how long they made me do it. It will seem like the longest 45 minutes of your life waiting for it attain the color of medium-to-dark chocolate. One false move, with the fire too hot or by not constantly stirring, and you start over. The good news is you don't have to do it very often. Freeze it! Spoon the roux into sectons of an ice cube tray. When frozen, remove the cubes and repackage.

Who doesn't appreciate mashed potatoes or rice and gravy every now and then, or a hot turkey and gravy sandwich, lightly toasted? Like great loves, superb gravy is a rare thing. So, don't waste it. If you have the "makings" in the pork chop or chicken skillet but don't plan to use it at the time, go ahead and make some gravy; just freeze it. I assure you it will come in handy. Those delicious brown bits in the pan will be absolutely wonderful on homemade biscuits for a Sunday brunch. Sometimes you will see a greasy film on top of the gravy. No problem – lay a paper towel on top to absorb every bit of it.

Gravy should always be served hot. To keep it hot, pour it into an insulated coffee carafe. You can make it ahead of time this way, avoiding the last-minute hassle.

— S A U C E S —

You will want some brown and white sauces in the freezer as they can cut a good 15 minutes off cooking and cleanup time for any number of recipes. I freeze the sauces in pint and half-pint jars, but you can just as easily pour them into zipper bags and lay them flat on a cookie sheet to freeze. This last method is recommended for boaters, campers and RVers.

FREEZER WHITE SAUCE

INGREDIENTS

1/2 pound of butter
(no substitutes for best texture)
•
1 cup white or whole wheat flour
•
2 quarts whole milk or evaporated
skim milk

In large skillet heat butter slowly, gradually stirring in the flour. Continue cooking the roux at a slow boil for 8 to 10 minutes to mellow the flour. Gradually add milk, stirring with a whisk to prevent lumping until sauce begins to thicken. Chill and freeze.

Depending on likely uses, half the liquid can be chicken, fish or vegetable broth. For best flavor, hold off adding cheese, tomato sauce or spices until ready to use the sauce in various recipes.

FREEZER BROWN SAUCE

No self-respecting chef would do it this way, but it's a good substitute. Brown sauce is such a time-consuming bother that it truly pays to make a large batch. Unfortunately, I've found nothing that can replace it. You can do Part I by itself and freeze it in small amounts. Or, you can take it all the way to a completed sauce.

Part I-Brown Sauce Base: In a large iron pot or skillet, measure equal amounts of chopped carrots, celery and onion – say 2 to 4 cups of each. Slowly sauté the vegetables in a small amount of unsalted butter until browned, tender and rich-tasting. If desired, add pepper, a sprinkle of nutmeg or ground bay leaf, and a teaspoon of thyme or oregano. Over high heat, add enough sherry,

Madeira or vermouth to the skillet to allow scraping up the flavorful vegetable bits. This is called deglazing. When deglazed, remove from skillet and cool. Freeze in half-pint jars or proceed to Part II.

Part II: Thaw a cup of brown sauce base in a skillet. Add 1/2 cup beef, pork or veal drippings and heat. Add 1/2 cup flour, incorporating quickly into sauce. Cook, stirring, until flour is nicely blended. At this point, you can go in various directions based on the end use. You will at the minimum be adding a quart of flavored stock to cook down to about half the volume. Refer to your cookbooks for ways to vary the sauce.

—BABY FOOD—
(HOMEMADE)

When my children were babies, I dabbled a little into preparing their food from vegetables and meat I'd cooked at home, but we couldn't afford much fresh food at the time. Thinking the way I do now about "ingredient" cooking, here's what I'd do.

With each supply of fresh vegetables, a portion would be set aside for the baby food. It would be steamed, then whirled in the blender. For this I'd use spinach, carrots, potatoes, peas, yams, beets, turnips, squash, broccoli, cauliflower – whatever was available, including tasty mixtures of two or more veggies. The same procedure would be used for chicken, veal, pork, ham and fish, adding chicken broth or other liquid as needed.

For fruits, I would use the Smoothie recipes, using a variety of fruits with milk, juice or yogurt. The puree recipes listed in this book would also be used. My children would eat a lot more nutritiously today than they could have back in the '60s.

Now, how can you store your vitamin-packed homemade baby food the easy way? Once again, call on your freezer for help. You can pour it into recycled baby food jars (immaculate ones, that is), pour it into ice cube trays, then to zipper bags, or into non-stick muffin tins to be repackaged when frozen. The frozen cubes or "muffins" can be microwaved right in baby's bowl. So convenient and so healthful.

You do want to identify the contents, though. If labeling is too much trouble, put different colored sticky dots on the vegetables, meats and fruits. (You don't want Junior to get a dose of pureed jalapeño pepper by mistake.) After the baby is eating table food, you'll have a jump on the college fund with the money you saved.

FRUITS

INTRODUCTION

It is easier than you might think to consume the recommended two to five servings of fruit every day. Fruit Smoothies are one of the easiest, further described in this section, and an ideal way to start the day. Most fruits contain fewer than 100 calories per cup – only bananas, papayas and pomegranates miss the mark, and not by much. In addition to their anti-carcinogenic compounds, fruits are loaded with Vitamins A, C and beta-carotene. They are rich in fiber and also provide potassium, iron, magnesium and calcium.

The keeping quality of fruits is somewhat less than vegetables. Store most varieties in the refrigerator (once ripened), a cool garage or basement while consuming them fresh. Individual fruit listings give you other options.

If you live in farm country, you know more than I about how to store large quantities of produce. However, today most of us buy rather than grow what we consume. If you live in a rural area and are fortunate enough to have a root cellar, crawl space or cool, humid cellar, you can store apples and pears for months. Granny Smith is one of the best keeping apple varieties. It is important to store such fruits away from vegetables, however, as they emit gases that can cause vegetables to sprout. Apples and pears also absorb odors from vegetables such as cabbage, Brussels sprouts and turnips. Any fruit you store in a root cellar must be in good condition.

The best cold storage temperatures are in the 32° to 40°F range, or close to freezing without letting anything freeze. Humidity should be between 80% and 90%. This humidity level keeps the fruit from shriveling up. The only way to monitor the humidity levels is with a hygrometer, available from hardware stores. If the level is too low, you can use a sprinkler or set out pans of water in the storage area.

Freezing fruits: See individual listings.

Thawing and using frozen fruits: Keep in mind that, because most fruits are frozen without blanching, microorganisms in the fruit begin reviving themselves during thawing. Don't take chances. Remove dry-packed fruits from freezer container and thaw in the refrigerator; use as soon as possible. Purees and syrup-packed fruits should be thawed in their original containers either in the refrigerator, quick-thawed in the microwave, or over hot water for immediate use. Fruits for sauces and Smoothies need not be defrosted before using.

FRUIT-YOGURT ICE CREAM

In Mexico I make ice cream regularly, taking advantage of fruit right from the trees. (I can't remember ever picking fruit from a tree in Alaska.) You don't need an ice cream maker – it will work fine frozen in ice trays or a large, flat bowl. Just about any fruit can be used, including a mixture of more than one. My favorites are pineapple, peach or nectarine, banana, orange, strawberry, blueberry, mango and papaya, and I usually do use fruit combinations. When each fruit is in season, I puree and freeze it in zipper bags, thus assuring a handy variety. Custard is the basis for any flavor of ice cream you choose, and it can be made well ahead of time and stored, covered, in the refrigerator. The custard doesn't have to be thick, which makes me happy since mine sometimes fails to thicken.

CUSTARD INGREDIENTS

1 quart milk
•
1 1/4 cups sugar
•
3" piece vanilla bean or 1 1/2 teaspoon vanilla
•
5 large egg yolks
•
1 1/4 cups cream

Heat milk, the vanilla and half of the sugar, stirring constantly, until milk begins bubbling around the edges of pan. In a bowl, beat sugar and egg yolks with wire whisk. Add about a half cup of the hot milk, stirring quickly, then pour the milk-sugar-egg yolk mixture back into the pan with remaining milk. Keep stirring until custard coats the back of a metal spoon. Remove from heat and stir in the cream. If using vanilla bean, scrape out the seeds and add to the custard. Chill until ready to make ice cream. You will have enough custard for two batches of ice cream.

YOGURT ICE CREAM INGREDIENTS

1 1/4 cup chopped pureed fruit or frozen fruit puree
•
1 1/2 cups sugar
•
3 cups custard
•
1 cup milk
•
1 1/2 cups plain or fruit-flavored yogurt

Heat fruit in a saucepan with the sugar, cooking until sugar is dissolved, five to ten minutes. Chill thoroughly, then add remaining ingredients. Pour into ice trays or flat bowl and freeze. Cover surface with plastic film. When frozen, remove from freezer and break up the mixture with a heavy metal spoon. Stir until smooth, then refreeze. This dissolves ice crystals and assures a smooth end product. You can do this twice if you like. Remove the ice cream a few minutes before serving to soften it properly.

Variations: Substitute orange juice for all or part of the milk or, if the mixture is too sweet, add lemon or lime juice. Pureed oranges go well with many fruits.

SERVES 8.

—APPLES—

Select a case of fresh-smelling, firm Granny Smith or other all-purpose apples. Store them wherever you have a cool, dark place. Lay newspaper loosely over the box to keep light away. If possible, spread them out so they're not touching, which helps air circulation. Check every few days to be sure none shows signs of spoilage; remove any that are bruised. To extend the life of apples, keep them in the refrigerator in a bag containing "breathing holes." A little more trouble to zip them up, but worth it.

Refresh tired apples by chopping and soaking them a few minutes in chilled apple juice. Also, remember to place apples as you cut them into cold water with a dash of lemon juice or ascorbic acid (Fruit Fresh, for example) to keep them from turning brown.

After eating your fill of them "as is," then what? Let them shrivel up to mere shadows of their former selves? You wouldn't. You have lots of options for using these high-quality, healthful fruits. Luscious pies, Waldorf salad, applesauce, apple butter, apple crisps, dumplings, fritters, or simply bake or fry them.

I got into the homemade applesauce thing by accident. A skillet of fried apples cooked too long and became "applesauce." So I tried doing it on purpose; besides, neither the taste nor the texture of commercial applesauce can match your own. My success then led to apple butter experiments. Both are as easy as mashed potatoes, and you can be just as flexible with the seasonings.

HOMEMADE APPLESAUCE

INGREDIENTS

Six or eight all-purpose apples
•
1/2 to 1 cup water or orange juice
•
Lemon juice to taste
•
Sugar, optional
•
Cinnamon, nutmeg, cloves or allspice

Put quartered, unpeeled (seeded and cored) apples with water or orange juice in a saucepan. Simmer until tender – about 20 minutes, adding more liquid if needed. Add lemon or sugar based on sweetness of apples and whirl in a blender. The skins will disappear, but not the vitamins in them. If you like, add a dash of cinnamon, nutmeg, cloves or allspice to the sauce.

That's all there is to it. Freeze in pint jars, leaving an inch of headroom. Applesauce keeps weeks in the refrigerator, fresh or frozen and thawed. Put a jar of freshly thawed applesauce on the table at breakfast or brunch for a refreshing treat.

HOMEMADE APPLE BUTTER

Use this guideline for any amount of apples. Cook apples as for applesauce. First, prepare a test cup. Remove one cup of the applesauce and stir in 2 teaspoons of cider vinegar. Note how much of the following ingredients you add to the cup, tasting after each addition: dark brown sugar, cinnamon, nutmeg and allspice. The apple butter should be medium to dark brown in color. I often add grated lemon peel to the test cup. When it tastes right, multiply the seasonings based on the amount of apples you have. Whirl the seasonings and apples in the blender until smooth. Adjust seasonings if necessary. Refrigerate some and freeze the rest in pint canning jars, leaving an inch of headroom.

APPLE PIES

Method 1. Using your favorite apple pie recipe, partially cook and freeze the fillings separately in quart-size zipper bags for several apple pies. When you want a pie, partially thaw a package of filling, put it into a prepared piecrust, and bake.

Method 2. Some cooks go one step further by laying foil or plastic wrap in a pie tin and freezing just the filling. Then they remove it from the pan and repackage the frozen pan-shaped filling. Take your choice. This freeze-it-in-a-pie-pan (and bake the frozen filling) method is very handy for last-minute company.

GRANNY'S BLACK WALNUT APPLESAUCE CAKE

*My grandmother shared many cooking techniques, more by example than overt lessons.
This family favorite was made with apples from our trees, although I don't know what variety they were. The black walnuts
came from a tree across the road. I'll never forget the scent of black walnuts lying in a pile of decaying leaves.
A neighbor cracked the nearly impervious shells for us. My grandmother and I would sit on the porch peeling apples – I
dreading all the while that a life-threatening worm would wiggle out, a common occurrence in those days before pesticides.*

INGREDIENTS

1 cup thick, tart applesauce (yours)
•
1 1/2 cups dark brown sugar
•
1/2 cup shortening or butter
•
1 egg
•
1 teaspoon *each* baking soda, salt and
cinnamon
•
1 3/4 cups flour, sifted
•
1 cup black walnuts, chopped
•
1/2 cup raisins
•
1/2 teaspoon clove
•
1/4 teaspoon allspice

Beat shortening, egg and sugar together, then add applesauce. Add dry ingredients, mixing well. Dust nuts and raisins first with flour to keep them from sinking to bottom of batter. The batter should be fairly stiff. Add more flour if necessary. Pour into a greased loaf or Bundt pan. Bake in preheated 350 degree oven about an hour. Serve with or without frosting.

PUREED APPLES FOR SMOOTHIES *

Cook fresh apples until soft, blend with water or orange juice, and freeze. Add 1/2 to 1 cup of apple puree to blender with other Smoothie ingredients. Example: Apple puree, banana, orange and juice, peach yogurt and ice cubes.

Apple puree should be a standard Smoothie ingredient. It blends superbly with most uncooked fruit purees, yogurt, milk, fruit juices and other beverages. If you are not a Smoothie aficionado, you're missing out on some unique taste treats.

*What is a SMOOTHIE? Just about anything you want it to be – made from fresh or frozen fruit, juice, yogurt, chocolate or plain milk, diet mixes, water or ice, whatever fruity concoction you dream up – whirled in a blender.

Smoothies provide an "instant" vitamin, mineral, fiber, amino-acid jolt in the morning or for snacks, and every blend is different, depending upon what you have on hand. Vitamins in pill form go down easily with a swallow of your Smoothie.

115

BAKED APPLES GALORE

Wash and remove cores of apples to be baked. Try not to cut clear to the bottom so the liquid stays intact, but it's OK if you do. Put a little water in the bottom of a baking dish and set apples inside.

Spoon one of these filling combinations in each apple and bake at about 350 degrees until tender, about half an hour, longer for large apples. Serve with juice from the baking dish or whipped cream.

Brown sugar and cinnamon
•
Honey and lemon juice
•
Cinnamon "red hots"
•
Toasted pine nuts
•
Preserves, marmalades or jam
•
Raisins or currants, and nuts
•
Fresh berries or bananas

—BANANAS—

Even though bananas are usually the least expensive fruit, I often wonder how families can afford them, especially at around a dollar a pound in many communities. Today, since the warehouse stores came to town, there's always a supply of perfect bananas in my Alaska kitchen, at about half the usual cost. And there are so many fine uses for them as is – cereal and bananas, bananas and cream, bananas mixed with pineapple, berries, melons, etc., in a compote, bananas in gelatin – even banana splits for a fabulous dessert.

Select a big bunch of the greenest bananas from the warehouse and ripen them at home. To speed up the process, put them in a paper bag stashed under the kitchen sink where it's nice and warm. To slow down their ripening, separate the green ones from the ripe ones. Once ripe, they can be refrigerated. The skins will darken, but that doesn't hurt the banana. They will keep even longer if you refrigerate them airtight in zipper bags. Freeze some whole or pureed for bread, ice cream or cake recipes.

BANANA PUREE ("MUFFINS") FOR THE FREEZER

I prefer freezing bananas by mashing them, adding lemon juice or Fruit Fresh to prevent darkening, and flash-freezing mounds of the puree in muffin tins. When the mounds are hard, remove from the tins to zipper bags. We call these "banana muffins," and they are a primary ingredient in breakfast Smoothies. Pop them in the blender with other fruits, purees or juices, and yogurt or milk. Store your leftover Smoothies in a covered jar in the refrigerator. During the day when you need a lift, shake the jar and have a drink. Kids like the banana "muffins" frozen as a snack.

If you like banana bread, measure the mashed banana into 1 cup mounds, and it's ready for making bread any time you are. This one is quick and easy.

BANANA BREAD

INGREDIENTS

1/2 cup butter
•
1/2 cup sugar
•
1 egg
•
2 cups flour
•
1 tablespoon baking powder
•
1/2 teaspoon nutmeg
•
2 cups ripe banana, mashed
•
1 teaspoon vanilla
•
1/2 cup raisins
•
1/2 cup chopped nuts

Beat butter and sugar together until light and fluffy. Add egg, beating thoroughly. Sift flour, baking powder and nutmeg into separate bowl. Alternate adding the flour mixture and bananas to the butter, sugar and egg mixture. Beat well after each addition to thoroughly blend. Sprinkle raisins lightly with flour and add raisins and nuts to batter, mixing again.

Grease a 9 x 5-inch loaf pan. Pour batter in; bake the bread in a 350-degree oven for 50-60 minutes or until toothpick inserted comes out clean.

SAUTÉED BANANAS

Cut 4 firm bananas lengthwise, then crosswise. Dip in 1/4 cup lemon juice, then roll in crumbs (bread, cracker, cookie) or ground nuts. Over medium-high heat, sauté in 2 tablespoons melted butter until browned, the faster the better to avoid overcooking the bananas. Serve as is or top with powdered sugar or lemon sauce (see Lemon Sauce recipe).

SERVES 4.

BANANA SLUSH

Here's an excellent drink using bananas that have reached perfect ripeness.
If you make it ahead of time, add the lemon-lime soda just before serving.

INGREDIENTS

3 ripe bananas (3 cups)
•
2 cups sugar
•
3 cups water
•
3 cups pineapple juice
•
1 1/2 cups orange juice
•
2 tablespoons lemon juice
•
1 quart lemon-lime soda
•
1/4 cup peach schnapps (optional)

Combine sugar and water in a saucepan. Boil five minutes and cool. In glass or plastic bowl mash bananas, adding the juices and cooled sugar water. Stir well and freeze in the bowl. Remove from freezer two hours before serving to let the mixture become slushy. Refrigerate or partially freeze again if it gets too slushy. At serving time, stir in lemon-lime soda and peach schnapps. Garnish glasses with mint sprig.

MAKES 12 SERVINGS.

BLAZING BANANAS

Recently a friend did the flaming thing at a luncheon in Alamos and caught the tablecloth on fire. Luckily there was a fountain nearby and the guests became the volunteer fire department with their drinking glasses.

INGREDIENTS

6 small bananas

•

Lemon, lime or orange juice

•

4 tablespoons butter

•

1 tablespoon brown sugar

•

4 tablespoons Grand Marnier
or Triple Sec

•

4 tablespoons dark rum or cognac

Peel and slice bananas lengthwise. Sprinkle with lemon, lime or orange juice to prevent browning and set aside. Melt butter in a skillet large enough to hold the bananas and add brown sugar. Add Grand Marnier or Triple Sec and rum, cognac or other compatible liqueur that will ignite. Now add the bananas. When the liqueurs are bubbly around the end of the pan (about a minute), hold a lighted match above the pan to ignite. This is a showy dessert, but for a dinner party, you might do a trial run. Any leftover sauce is delicious heated with a little fresh orange juice and served over crepes or French toast.

SERVES 6.

BANANA SALSA SUPREME

The colors and sweet-sour flavors make this a memorable accompaniment to fish or fowl; and it's a refreshing salsa for tortilla chips. By the way, fruit salsas are becoming more and more popular. I've never served one that wasn't a conversation piece. This newspaper recipe originally appeared in Steven Raichlen's Miami Spice. Make just enough for one meal or appetizer as it doesn't keep well. The chopping can be done earlier, but hold the bananas until one or two hours before serving.

INGREDIENTS

2 large bananas, diced

•

1/2 large green bell pepper, diced

•

1/2 large red bell pepper, diced

•

1 tablespoon fresh ginger root, grated

•

3 or 4 green onions, including tops,
finely sliced

•

3 tablespoons fresh or frozen lime juice

•

2 tablespoons dark brown sugar

•

1 tablespoon olive oil

•

Salt and freshly ground pepper

Combine all ingredients and adjust seasonings. Cover surface with plastic film and refrigerate. Serve with tortilla chips.

SERVES 4-6.

BANANA PINEAPPLE SALAD

This is such a pretty salad, it can dress up any table. Simple, but very refreshing. Cut large peeled bananas in half, then once lengthwise. Put two slices on lettuce leaves on each plate, crossing one banana slice over the other. Cut one slice of canned pineapple and twist it into an "S" shape over the bananas. On each side of the banana arrange fresh strawberries, kiwi slices, cherries or orange sections. Top with a honey dressing or spoonful of sour cream.

BAKED BANANAS WITH BRANDIED RAISINS

This great recipe came from a magazine called Baja Life.
Food writer Kay Pastorius says she keeps a jar of raisins covered with brandy on hand for desserts such as this.
The brandy keeps the raisins indefinitely. Pastorius also recommends soaking them in Amaretto or rum.

INGREDIENTS

3 tablespoons brown sugar
•
3/4 cup chopped walnuts
•
3/4 cup brandy-soaked raisins
•
4 firm bananas, peeled and cut lengthwise
•
2 tablespoons unsalted butter

Place bananas in a buttered baking dish. Sprinkle with sugar, raisins and nuts. Dot with butter. Bake at 350 degrees for 25 minutes or until lightly browned.

SERVES 4 OR 8.

— BERRIES —

The warehouses carry 5-pound bags of frozen strawberries and blueberries, which are wonderful to have in the freezer for Smoothies, ice cream, and for serving "as is." Sometimes they carry an excellent blend of raspberries, blackberries, blueberries and strawberries. This combination is my standard "emergency" dessert. I sprinkle sugar over several cups of the berries, top them with Bisquick, and pop the dish in the oven for 20 minutes.

BERRIES AND "CREAM"

An instant low-calorie dessert I serve frequently consists simply of frozen berries blended into low- or non-fat whipped topping. I put the berries and topping in stemmed glasses, cover each with plastic film and refrigerate until dessert time. Or, live it up with the real thing.

— S T R A W B E R R I E S —

When strawberries are upwards of $2.50 a pint at the supermarket, I have no trouble convincing myself how enjoyable a flat from the warehouse would be. In fact, I've been known to eat the whole thing myself over several days. Selecting good strawberries is easy. They should smell heavenly, be bright red and not exhibit bruising or mold. You can actually pick out a flat that no "middle man" has touched since the grower packed it, thus assuring less damage to these delicate marvels. They'd best be ripe, because what you see is what you get.

Not to be passed by are the 5-pound bags of frozen strawberries. The cream of the crop is selected for freezing, and strawberries are up there with bananas as favored ingredients for Smoothies. Since Smoothies are best served ice cold, it is actually better to place fruits such as strawberries in the blender frozen.

I've tried every trick to make fresh strawberries last longer; here are the most successful and convenient.

Fresh Strawberry Saver #1: Rinse, then hull berries. Cover a platter with paper toweling. Arrange the strawberries on it, cut side down, and stretch plastic film tightly over the berries and platter. Refrigerate. Every time you open the fridge, remove the platter and indulge.

Fresh Strawberry Saver #2: Wash and let unhulled strawberries dry on paper towels. Gently place the berries in a large jar with paper toweling at the bottom to absorb any liquid. Cover tightly and refrigerate until you need a strawberry "fix."

Remember this rule when serving strawberries: "Wash first, then remove stems." This way the juice and flavor stay with the berries.

Most Scrumptious Way to Eat Strawberries
Dip strawberries in sour cream,
then in brown sugar. Eat.

Second Most Scrumptious Way to Eat Strawberries
Marinate a few minutes in balsamic vinegar.

S T R A W B E R R Y   S A U C E

In the unlikely event you have fresh berries left, do this: For an ice cream or cake topping, slice a pint of fresh strawberries into a saucepan. Add two tablespoons of strawberry jam, a little powdered sugar, if needed, and a teaspoon of balsamic vinegar. Freeze for later use or simmer just to blend flavors. Serve the sauce warm or cold over fruit, ice cream or cake. You can also make this sauce with frozen berries. Just about any kind of berry makes a great sauce in minutes.

STRAWBERRY SODA BASE

INGREDIENTS

1 quart (4 cups) fresh strawberries, washed and hulled

•

2 cups sugar

•

1 cup water

•

1 teaspoon lemon juice

In a saucepan, bring sugar and water to a boil, stirring until sugar dissolves. Add lemon juice and strawberries, simmering for about 15 minutes. When cool, puree in blender. Refrigerate, covered, a week or two or freeze in convenient portions. (I use Frappuccino bottles.) When serving the sodas, figure about two ounces of strawberry base for each glass. Fill 10-ounce glasses with equal amounts of club soda and milk. Serve with straws.

STRAWBERRY SMOOTHIE

INGREDIENTS

1 cup frozen strawberries

•

1/2 cup fruit-flavored yogurt

•

1/2 cup orange juice

STUFFED STRAWBERRIES

A light, colorful appetizer.

INGREDIENTS

12 large strawberries of uniform size

•

2 ounces low-fat cream cheese

•

1-2 tablespoons real or imitation sour cream

•

Brown sugar

Remove stems from strawberries. Cut each one from tip almost to the stem with a + cut. Spread the berry slightly to hold filling. Mix the cream cheese and sour cream and fill the berries. Sprinkle with brown sugar.

SERVES 6 AS AN APPETIZER.

—BLUEBERRIES—

A large carton of fresh blueberries at the height of the season means a treat all winter long for the plan-ahead warehouse shopper. Better yet, buy two. Suppose you're too busy the day you bring them home to prepare for their ultimate uses. Not to worry. Just spread them on a cookie sheet and freeze until hard. Bag them up and you're set for winter. In virtually any recipe, blueberries can be used fresh or frozen. Here are some nice options.

BLUEBERRY FROZEN YOGURT

INGREDIENTS

2 cups blueberries

•

1/3 cup honey

•

2 cups plain yogurt, or
half plain and half blueberry-flavored yogurt

In an enamel or stainless steel pan, cook the blueberries and honey for five minutes. Refrigerate until cold. Put mixture in blender and process until smooth. Fold in yogurt, then pour into two ice cube trays or a square cake pan. Cover with foil and freeze until firm, 3 to 4 hours.

Break the frozen mixture into chunks and pour into a chilled mixing bowl. Beat until fluffy (this steps eliminates the ice crystals) and pour back into freezer container. Refreeze until firm, or several hours. Remove about 5 minutes before serving to soften the dessert. For company I usually fill the dessert dishes and set them on a tray in the freezer. That way you're not away from guests but a few seconds.

SERVES 8.

BLUEBERRY BUCKLE

I have no idea what a "buckle" is, nor do I know where another family recipe called "Blueberry Grunt" originated.
You'll enjoy this, even if you choose to give it a more glamorous name.

INGREDIENTS

1/2 cup sugar
•
2 cups flour
•
2 1/2 teaspoons baking powder
•
1/4 teaspoon salt
•
1 egg
•
1/2 cup milk
•
1/4 cup melted butter
•
2 cups blueberries

Mix sugar, flour, baking powder and salt in a bowl. Make a well in the flour mixture and add the egg, milk and butter. Beat all together just enough to form a dough, then pour into a greased square glass baking dish. Pour blueberries over..

TOPPING

1/2 cup light brown sugar
•
1/4 cup butter
•
1/3 cup flour
•
1/2 teaspoon cinnamon

With two knives, cut the butter into the dry ingredients. It will be lumpy. Sprinkle over blueberries and bake 40-50 minutes at 350 degrees.

BLUEBERRY SMOOTHIE

For this colorful Smoothie, blend 1/2 cup frozen blueberries with 1/2 cup skim milk, 1/2 banana and 1 tablespoon honey.

Keep frozen blueberries handy to toss into other fruit Smoothies.

—CHERRIES—

Cherry season is all too short, and crop failures can make it even shorter. Grab a carton at the warehouse and eat them as is 'til your heart's content. The smooth, purple to black Bing cherries are ripe when you buy them, so refrigerate them quickly. Pit and freeze some for Smoothies-just toss them in a jar, and use some for a great dessert or two.

CHERRY COBBLER WITH AMARETTO CREAM

INGREDIENTS

2 tablespoons cornstarch
•
1 cup water
•
1 pound fresh cherries, pitted
(about 2 cups)
•
2 teaspoons grated lemon peel
•
1/4 cup sugar
•
1/4 teaspoon salt
•
1/2 teaspoon almond flavoring

In a saucepan, mix together the water and cornstarch. Add cherries, lemon, sugar and salt. Cook, stirring until thickened; remove from heat and add almond flavoring. Pour the mixture into a buttered 8" square baking dish.

TOPPING

1/2 cup all-purpose flour
•
3/4 teaspoon baking powder
•
1/4 teaspoon salt
•
1 tablespoon sugar
•
2 tablespoons soft butter
•
1 egg
•
2 tablespoons milk

Lightly blend flour, baking powder, salt, sugar, butter, milk and egg. Spoon batter over the cherry mixture. Bake in 350-degree oven about 20 minutes to brown the crust. Serve with Amaretto cream.

AMARETTO CREAM
Mix 3 tablespoons of amaretto liqueur into 1 cup sour cream.

BETTY CATO'S FRUIT PIZZA

The late Betty Cato, a colorful Alaska legislator, could always be counted on to find fresh or frozen berries for her favorite potluck dish. Easy, attractive and refreshing, but eat it all – this dish doesn't keep.

INGREDIENTS

17-ounce roll refrigerated sugar
cookie dough

•

8-ounce package cream cheese,
softened

•

1/3 cup sugar

•

1/2 teaspoon vanilla

•

Bing cherries, fresh or frozen, halved

•

Whole strawberries, fresh or frozen,
halved lengthwise

•

Blueberries and peach slices, fresh or
frozen

•

Mandarin oranges, canned

•

1/4 cup orange marmalade mixed with
1 tablespoon water

Line a 14-inch pizza pan or similar-sized pan with foil. Slice cookie dough into 1/8-inch slices and arrange them on the pan to form a crust. Bake in preheated 375-degree oven for 10 minutes or until lightly browned. When cooled, lift away from foil and replace in pan or on serving dish.

Mix the cream cheese, sugar and vanilla until well blended and spread over crust. Arrange fruit decoratively in circles on top. Cover with marmalade-water mixture and refrigerate. Cut into 12 wedges. Chill until ready to serve.

—GRAPEFRUIT—

I thought it was Christmas the first time I saw a display of glorious pink grapefruit at Costco. Without even wondering what to do with it, a case found its way to my shopping cart. The fruit was plump, heavy, firm and thin-skinned, which meant it would be sweet, juicy and meaty.

My biggest problem was finding room for it in the refrigerator. For several days the covered case stayed in my cool garage. Then about a dozen of them were packed in zipper bags in the refrigerator. We had broiled grapefruit. Tequila and grapefruit juice cocktails. Grapefruit salad dressing. Grapefruit halves for breakfast. Grapefruit sections in salads. Grapefruit served with peach schnapps. Some was frozen as juice (just squeeze and freeze). It wasn't long before, alas, they vanished.

GRAPEFRUIT AND AVOCADO SALAD

Peel and carefully section 2 grapefruit. Peel and slice two avocados lengthwise and sprinkle with lemon juice. Arrange on leaf or head lettuce on four salad plates. Sprinkle with sliced green onions and chopped walnuts or pine nuts. Cover with a dressing made of good olive oil, rice wine vinegar, salt and pepper.

SERVES 4.

DRUNKEN GRAPEFRUIT

Cut three grapefruit in half and remove the centers with a grapefruit knife. Loosen each section. Place the fruit halves in a baking dish and pour a teaspoon or more of sherry or Madeira wine over each. Cover each of the tops with a tablespoon of brown sugar and a small piece of butter. Bake at 375 degrees until heated through and lightly browned, about 20 minutes. To serve, decorate each half with a maraschino cherry and a sprig of mint.

SERVES 6.

—LEMONS AND LIMES—

If there is one food-enhancing ingredient a cook cannot live without, it has to be the lemon. Its virtues are too many to extol, as are the times a lemon has saved what might have been a disastrous dish. Too sweet? Add lemon. Too boring? Add lemon. Too greasy? Add lemon. Too salty? Add lemon. You get the picture. Because lemons are loaded with Vitamin C, a known cancer inhibitor, juice or grated rind should be added last when cooking. Heat destroys this vitamin.

What can you do with a 5-pound bag of lemons? That question stumped me for a while. Finally I succumbed and bought a bag, which was easy since I had been buying lemons for 89 cents each. The first bag presented a challenge, but not an insurmountable one.

I soon discovered the secret. Lemons can easily last two months if refrigerated in plastic zipper bags. In fact, I tested their lifespan by putting half my supply in zipper bags and storing the rest in the vegetable bin. You can guess which lasted far longer. The results of that test encouraged me to store as much citrus fruit as possible the same way. If you repeated the test, you too would be a believer.

128

INSTANT LEMON FLAVOR

(1) Grate the yellow part only from six or eight lemons. Flash freeze on a flat surface; then pour into a small jar. Keep handy in freezer door.

(2) Squeeze the juice from the same lemons, remove the seeds and freeze the juice in small jars or ice cube trays. Thaw only what you need, returning remainder to freezer.

(3) Simplify the process for certain end uses. Grate the lemon peel, extract the juice and combine the two in small jars (baby food or spice jars) before freezing. I find the peel retains its intense flavor better with this method. Since many recipes call for both grated peel and juice, this is handy – all you need is a tea strainer to separate them for measuring.

(4) Make "lemony" sugar to sprinkle on dishes needing a little zest. For two cups of sugar, add two tablespoons of fresh or frozen grated lemon rind. Shake and store in a covered jar.

(5) Slice lemons crosswise, freeze on a cookie sheet, then repack into jars. Use the frozen slices in punches, to decorate fruit or salad plates, and to float in soup bowls.

There's no need to let your supply of lemons shrivel up and spoil. Remember that old adage, "When the world hands you a lemon, make lemonade." You can have "fresh" lemonade any time with your own syrup.

SYRUP FOR LEMONADE

(1) Grate the rind of two lemons – just the yellow part
(2) Squeeze the pulp and juice from six lemons
(3) Boil a cup of sugar in 1/4 cup of water

When the sugar water reaches the thread stage (makes a thin thread when spooned above the pan), add the juice and grated rind from the lemons. Let it cook a while, bringing to just below the boiling point. Pour the liquid through a tea strainer into an ice cube tray. Chill first, then freeze. Toss the frozen lemonade cubes into a plastic zipper bag or glass jar. Put one cube in a glass, add water and ice and there's your "fresh" lemonade when you want it. A sprig of mint tops it off nicely.

REALLY FRESH LEMONADE

Squeeze the juice from enough lemons to equal one cup. Boil 2 cups of sugar in a quart of water. Remove from heat. Add the lemon juice. Cool and pour over ice in tall glasses. Garnish with mint or fresh fruit.

SERVES 4.

On a muggy, buggy North Carolina afternoon, this visiting Alaskan was treated to an exquisite lemon ice served in a lemon shell. My host said she selects perfect lemons, cuts them crosswise in half, removes the pulp and refrigerates the shells in cold water for up to two days. (Italian ices are often served this way.)

The lemon shells can just as easily be frozen. I've used the shells to hold cocktail sauce on a seafood platter, salsa for Mexican eggs, and for warm lemon butter alongside fresh green asparagus or baked fish. Guests think this is really nifty. Sometimes just a little touch like this elevates an ordinary meal to a special one.

LEMON ICE IN LEMON CUPS

INGREDIENTS

2 cups sugar
•
2 1/2 teaspoons grated lemon rind
•
4 cups water
•
Pinch of salt
•
3/4 cup fresh or frozen lemon juice

Put sugar into a saucepan with grated lemon rind (white part only). Add 4 cups of water and salt. Heat to the boiling point, stirring until sugar is dissolved. Cover the pot and boil gently for five minutes without stirring to avoid crystallizing the mixture. Chill and stir in 3/4 cup of fresh lemon juice. Pour into a heavy-duty plastic freezer bag and freeze until slushy. About every half hour, remove the bag and pound it with a mallet or massage it well to break up the ice crystals (I know this sounds strange, but it works). When the mixture is ready, spoon it into lemon shells on a tray covered with plastic film. Cover and keep frozen until just before serving.

SERVES 8.

LEMON CURD

This wonderful sauce can be used for lemon tarts, cookies, as a filling for many cakes, or as a spread.
Very handy to have around, and simple to make.

INGREDIENTS

1/2 cup butter

•

Juice of 4 lemons (about 1 cup juice)

•

1 tablespoon grated lemon peel

•

1 1/2 cups sugar

•

5 eggs, beaten

Melt butter in heavy saucepan. Add lemon juice, grated peel and sugar. Cook and stir until sugar dissolves. Pour a little of the heated mixture into beaten eggs, then return all back to the pan. Continue cooking until mixture thickens, 15 to 20 minutes. Cool and refrigerate. Spoon into half-pint lidded jars and store in refrigerator for up to 2 months, or in freezer.

—MANGOS—

Mangos are in season such a short time in the North that it's smart to take advantage of them. Ripen mangos at room temperature; they are ripe when the skin yields to firm pressure. Eat peeled, sliced mango (chilled) with fresh lime juice or with ice cream. Or, a real bargain is the 64-ounce jar of Sunfresh mango slices. Each jar contains the fruit of 10 to 14 mangoes. Mango puree is a grand way to preserve some of your supply, and you don't need to cook it first. Mango salsa is out of this world, wonderful as a meat and fish accompaniment, and always a refreshing alternative to guacamole with tortilla chips. Here are two favorites that may become yours.

MANGO PUREE FOR THE FREEZER

Peel and separate the fruit from the seed (can be messy), cut in chunks and blend at low speed until smooth. Add a little sugar and freeze in pint or half-pint jars. The puree is wonderful in fruit Smoothies, in ice cream, and in a light dessert such as this one.

MANGO VELVET

INGREDIENTS

1 large ripe mango (or about 3 cups frozen puree, thawed)

•

2 tablespoons fresh or frozen lemon juice

•

2 tablespoons honey

•

2 tablespoons dark brown sugar

•

1/4 teaspoon powdered ginger

•

1 cup whipped cream

•

1/4 cup *each* sliced almonds and coconut

Blend first five ingredients until smooth. Fold the blended mixture into whipped cream and spoon into four dessert cups. Chill. Toast sliced almonds and coconut in dry skillet, being careful not to burn. Sprinkle over the dessert when ready to serve.

MANGO TOMATILLO SALSA

From the Chile-Heads Recipe Collection came this unique combination.
I tried it just to use those little papery-covered green tomatoes that had piqued my curiosity.

INGREDIENTS

4 large ancho chiles, roasted

•

6 garlic cloves, mashed

•

3 ripe mangoes, diced

•

7 tomatillos, diced

•

8 plum tomatoes, diced

•

1 large white onion, diced

•

1 tablespoon vinegar

•

Juice of 2 limes

•

1 bunch fresh cilantro, chopped

Roast ancho chiles and garlic in oven. Remove chiles when they are puffed out, and the garlic when it is soft. Mix mangoes, tomatillos, tomatoes and onions in a large bowl. Add vinegar and lime juice, garlic and crumbled chiles. For hotter salsa, add the chile seeds. Mix in cilantro and chill several hours. You'll love it.

MANGO SALSA

2 ripe mangos, peeled and diced

•

3/4 cup fresh or frozen onion,
preferably red

•

1 fresh or frozen jalapeño pepper,
minced

•

1/4 to 1/2 cup fresh or frozen lime
juice

•

1 bunch fresh cilantro, chopped (up to
a cup)

•

1/4 cup fresh basil, chopped

•

Salt and freshly ground pepper to taste

This makes about four cups to serve chilled with tortilla chips. Mango slices from the Sunfresh jar also work well for making salsa any time of the year.

—ORANGES—

The cases of large, heavy, seedless oranges that tempt warehouse shoppers are the finest quality, shipped at the peak of perfection. Thin-skinned oranges generally are juicier than those with thick skins. Despite all precautions, soft or rotting orange may lurk in the box. Check carefully when you unpack them, then again in a day or so. Store them in the coolest place possible if refrigerator room is not available for your supply. As with other citrus fruit, immersing in hot water, zapping in the microwave or heating a few minutes in the oven makes oranges easier to peel.

ORANGES FOR THE FREEZER

Before they do their typical disappearing act, rescue a dozen or so oranges for future use. For orange puree, peel and quarter the oranges and whirl them in the blender. Freeze the puree for Smoothies, Roasted Orange and Yellow Pepper Soup (see recipe), homemade sherbets and ices. The fiber in your puree is nutritious and should be reserved even when you're squeezing oranges for juice. With a citrus zester remove strips of the skin and freeze in a small jar. It's also a good idea to slice some perfect seedless oranges for garnishes. I do this on a cookie sheet, then bag the slices.

One more thing you may wish to do with those perfectly colored oranges – use just the shells to hold fruits, salads, chilled soups and desserts. After cutting the oranges and carefully removing the fruit, use scissors or a sharp knife to decorate the shell, then freeze it. All these orange goodies keep for months, and you'll be glad to have them on hand.

ORANGE, ONION AND CILANTRO SALAD

Simple but elegant served on attractive salad plates, and so perfect with seedless Valencia oranges. Slice crosswise two large red onions. Peel and slice crosswise two oranges of equal size. Arrange the onions and oranges on a bed of lettuce on four salad plates. Mix 4 tablespoons of extra virgin olive oil with a tablespoon each of lemon and orange juice. Sprinkle fresh cilantro leaves over the tops.

SERVES 4.

BAKED BRANDIED ORANGES

Cover whole oranges with boiling water and simmer until skin is tender, about 10 minutes. Cut in half and, with a grapefruit knife, remove the center pithy core without cutting through to the bottom. Arrange in baking dish. Sprinkle tops and centers with sugar. Put a dollop of butter on each and a tablespooon of brandy or peach schnapps. Broil until bubbly and lightly browned.

ORANGE, AVOCADO AND CILANTRO SOUP (CHILLED)

There's just one way to know how good this soup is – try it.

INGREDIENTS

1 cup fresh orange juice
(or your frozen)
•
4-6 cups chicken broth
•
4 small or two large avocados
•
2 tablespoons fresh cilantro leaves
•
1 jalapeño pepper, chopped
•
1/4 cup tequila

Put ingredients in a pitcher and pour into blender 2 cups at a time. Blend until smooth, but not too thin. Chill. This soup is spectacular served in a half cantaloupe or the shells of grapefruit or oranges, decorated with mint or cilantro sprigs. Be sure to flatten the base of the "bowl" so it will sit level.

SERVES 8.

STEAMED ORANGE CUSTARD

INGREDIENTS

3 large strips orange peel
(colored part only) 3" x 3/4" each
•
One 2-inch piece vanilla bean
•
2 1/2 cups milk
•
2/3 cup sugar
•
3 egg yolks
•
1 large egg
•
1 tablespoon Cointreau or Grand
Marnier

SERVES 4.

Combine orange peel, vanilla bean and milk in saucepan. Heat, stirring, just until bubbly around the edge of pan, about 15 minutes. Remove and set aside to cool, about 30 minutes. In a medium-sized skillet heat half of the sugar (1/3 cup) without stirring until sugar begins to melt, about 5 minutes. Then begin stirring slowly until the sugar is completely melted and caramelized, another 5 minutes. Pour into four custard cups. Set aside.

In a large skillet or pan with lid, place a rack or inverted cake pan and add an inch of water. Bring to boil. Meanwhile whisk the eggs to blend and quickly stir in about half the cooled milk mixture. Add remaining milk, stirring to keep mixture smooth. (NOTE: If custard separates, whirl a few seconds in blender.) Remove orange peel and vanilla bean, and add remaining sugar and liqueur. Place cups on rack in skillet and cover tightly with plastic film. Cover and steam 20 minutes, without peeking. Then uncover and let cool in pan. Refrigerate. Loosen custard around edges and invert onto dessert plates. Decorate with orange slices or peel.

— PAPAYAS —

Selecting perfect papayas can be a bit tricky. If they are all green, pass them by – they were picked too soon and won't ripen. Look for a flat containing fruits that are reddish orange; a little green on them is OK. They should yield slightly to pressure. If they're too soft or bruised, don't buy them.

If more ripening is needed, put them in a paper bag with an apple and hold at room temperature. They'll last more than a week refrigerated in airtight zipper bags. Freeze chunks of papaya in a light syrup (1 3/4 cups sugar to 2 cups

water) or puree it. Either can be used in Smoothies or ice cream.

In Alamos our papaya tree bears fruit weighing up to ten pounds; they can grow up to 20 pounds. It always amuses me when recipes call for a papaya without indicating more precise measurements. That could get the cook in real trouble.

It's hard to beat papaya halves with lime juice, the simplest way to serve it. I also love it with fresh berries and/or yogurt ice cream. Mint leaves are the perfect garnish.

BAKED PAPAYA ALASKA

INGREDIENTS

2 medium-sized papayas, about 1 pound each

•

4 tablespoons butter

•

2 tablespoons fresh or frozen lime juice

•

1/2 teaspoon ground ginger

Cut papayas in half lengthwise and remove seeds. Cut thin slice off bottom to level the fruit. Place in greased foil-lined baking dish. Fill centers with butter, lime juice and ginger. Bake at 350 degrees for about 30 minutes. Use butter mixture to baste the fruit and continue cooking until tender. Chill.

4 egg whites
1/2 cup sugar
Vanilla ice cream

Beat egg whites and a dash of salt until stiff. Gradually beat in sugar until meringue is glossy. Put large scoop of hard vanilla ice cream in each papaya half and spread meringue over top to cover both. Immediately put in 500-degree oven to brown meringue, 2 or 3 minutes. Serve before the ice cream melts!

NOTE: It's a good idea to estimate how much ice cream each papaya "hole" will need; then freeze it in four nice-sized mounds on a cookie sheet. Time is of the essence here.

SERVES 4.

PAPAYA SLUSH

INGREDIENTS

2 cups frozen papaya slices

•

3 cups orange juice

•

3 cups ice water

•

Lemon juice to taste

•

Ice cubes

Combine papaya and orange juice in blender, blending until smooth. At high speed add 5-6 ice cubes and blend until mixture is slushy. Thin to desired consistency with cold water.

SERVES 6.

PAPAYA SALSA

Prepare as you would peach salsa – recipe in the following section.

—PEACHES AND NECTARINES—

Peach season is all too short where I live, so we eat them like crazy when we can. A case of perfect specimens from the warehouse stores isn't exactly cheap, but sometimes you just have to splurge. However, the case price always beats $2.99 - $3.99 a pound at the supermarket. Take care not to bruise them. Don't expect to buy your peaches ripe – they ripen perfectly well in a few days after you've laid them out at room temperature. Be sure they are ripe before you refrigerate them in plastic zipper bags.

Peaches and nectarines can be frozen sprinkled with sugar (2/3 cup per 4 cups fruit), by immersing slices in a light syrup, or pureeing them with a small amount of orange juice. For either method, sprinkle the fruit with Fruit Fresh or diluted lemon juice to prevent browning.

137

PEACH-ORANGE PUREE

Back when I was a less experienced cook, everything was done by the book – and that meant freezing fruit in syrup, using ascorbic acid, etc. By accident (the way we create many recipes), I found an easier, more healthful method. With a good supply of peaches and oranges on hand when I was leaving town, I had to do something, quick. This puree has since become a mainstay for our favorite fruit Smoothies. Do try this.

Put equal amounts of peach (or nectarine) and orange chunks in a blender, and puree. Pour into pint jars or bottles and freeze. These thaw overnight in the refrigerator and are ready to pour into the blender the next morning with bananas, yogurt or juice.

PEACH SALSA

Of all the fruit salsas I serve, this is the most popular. More often than not I use nectarines (actually a peach variety) which seem to me more reliable in quality than peaches. They also tend to be juicier.

INGREDIENTS

3 or 4 peaches or nectarines
•
1 tablespoon lime juice, fresh or frozen
•
2 tablespoons honey
•
1/4 cup cilantro, chopped
•
2 tablespoons red bell pepper, chopped
•
2 jalapeno peppers, minced
•
Salt and pepper to taste

Dice peaches or nectarines. Mix with lime juice, honey, chopped cilantro and peppers. Season with salt and pepper. If too sweet, add more lime juice. Cover surface with plastic film and chill. Good with tortilla chips, jicama slices or as an accompaniment to seafood and pork.

SERVES 4.

DIVINE PEACH HONEY

This easy concoction has the texture of jam.

INGREDIENTS

12 large peaches, peeled and pitted
•
1 large orange and peel
•
Sugar

Put orange, including peel, and peaches through a food chopper or chop small amounts at a time lightly in blender. Measure the mixture and add an equal amount of sugar. Cook until thick, about 20 minutes. Pour into hot sterilized pint jars; chill and store in the freezer. Serve on bread, broiled grapefruit or French toast. Also a welcome hostess gift.

MAKES 5 PINTS.

PEACH COBBLER

This is probably my favorite peach cobbler. Sometimes I add cooked rhubarb for a different touch.

INGREDIENTS

2 cups water
•
2 cups sugar
•
2 tablespoons cornstarch
•
6-7 peaches or nectarines, sliced
•
2 tablespoons butter
•
Cinnamon to taste
•
Lemon (optional)

Boil water, 2 cups sugar and cornstarch for one minute. Add sliced fruit. Add lemon if too sweet. Pour into baking dish and dot with butter and cinnamon.

TOPPING

1 cup flour
•
1 tablespoon sugar
•
1 1/2 teaspoon baking powder
•
1/2 teaspoon salt
•
3 tablespoons butter
•
1/2 cup milk or buttermilk

For topping, mix flour, sugar, baking powder, salt, butter and milk. Spread over peaches. Bake in 400-degree oven for 30 minutes until top is lightly browned.

KRIS'S KILLER PEACH GIN FREEZE

On a hot Anchorage summer evening, I first tasted this refreshing cocktail while waiting for our hosts' barbecued ribs. Dinner was a little late, and we "over-enjoyed" a few more. Good thing we could walk home!

INGREDIENTS

3 cups peaches or nectarines, peeled
•
9 ounces gin
•
3 ounces peach schnapps
•
Ice cubes

In a blender, puree peaches or nectarines. Add gin and peach schnapps. Divide the mixture in half and blend each half with 3 cups of cracked ice or cubes until slushy. Pour into four margarita or wine glasses.

SERVES 4.

PEACHES IN WINE

Such an easy dessert, and one you might want to add to your peach repertoire.

INGREDIENTS

4 cups peaches, sliced
•
2 cups dry white wine
•
3 tablespoons honey
•
3 tablespoons fresh mint, chopped
•
1/2 cup Amaretto liqueur
•
Cinnamon (optional)

Combine ingredients in a glass serving dish. Cover and refrigerate 4-6 hours. Dust lightly with cinnamon before serving.

SERVES 6-8.

—PEARS—

Select pears that appear smooth, firm (but not too hard), and free of bruises. They are shipped unripe because of their delicate skin, but continue ripening while in transit and in cold storage. Once ripe, pears are pleasantly scented and yield to slight pressure.

Treat them gently; they are one of the most perishable popular fruits. Do not refrigerate pears in airtight plastic bags; their ethylene gasses will cause rapid spoilage. Better to spread them loosely in your refrigerator produce bins.

The slightest bruise or cut will cause the skin to turn brown. Have lemon juice or Fruit Fresh on hand to protect them.

Two excellent serving suggestions for perfectly ripened pears (slice and sprinkle with anti-browning solution just before serving) are these: (1) Wrap pear slices with prosciutto and serve as a first course. (2) For dessert, accompany slices of unpeeled pear with slabs of Roquefort, Camembert or Brie and cheddar cheese.

PEARS IN WINE

INGREDIENTS

4 firm pears, unpeeled, with stems
•
4 whole cloves
•
1 cup red wine
•
1/2 cup water
•
1/2 cup sugar

Insert a clove in the blossom end of each pear. Lay whole pears lengthwise in a deep baking dish. Add wine, water and sugar. Cover. Bake at 400 degrees for 30 minutes, basting three times. Remove cover, continue basting, and bake about 15 minutes or until pears are tender. Serve hot or cold with wine sauce.

SERVES 4.

PEARS IN CHOCOLATE SAUCE

INGREDIENTS

4 pears, peeled

Juice of 1/2 lemon

1/2 cup sugar

1/4 teaspoon vanilla

4 ounces dark chocolate, grated

2 tablespoons heavy cream

1 tablespoon butter

1 tablespoon Kahlua or
créme de cacao

Maraschino cherries

Leave stems on peeled pears. Sprinkle thoroughly with lemon juice and set aside. Heat water and sugar in pan large enough to hold pears upright. When sugar is dissolved, add vanilla and pears, simmering over low heat about 15 minutes. Let cool in sugar water, then drain.

In a double boiler, melt chocolate; add cream, butter and liqueur. To serve, pour chocolate sauce over pears. Garnish with maraschino cherries.

SERVES 4.

POACHED PEARS, CHERRIES AND PRUNES

This combination of spices, fresh and dried fruit is subtle, sensuous and elegant.

INGREDIENTS

1 cup dried cherries

1 cup prunes

2 cups red wine

1 cup water

3/4 cup sugar

2 tablespoons lemon peel, chopped

4 peppercorns

4 cloves

1 cinnamon stick

4 pears, peeled and halved

Put all ingredients in a stainless steel, Pyrex or enamel-coated saucepan. Simmer for 10 minutes. Add pears and continue cooking until pears are soft but not mushy. Chill 8 hours or overnight. Serve at room temperature.

SERVES 4.

—PINEAPPLE—

You can't always tell a pineapple book by its cover. I've bought perfect-looking ones that were either too ripe or not ripe enough or had bad spots inside. If the fruit has a pronounced odor, it may be overripe and fermenting. With pineapples, you "pays your money and you takes your chances."

Select heavy, fragrant pineapples with a good orange color. The leafy center spines should be compact but easy to pull out. There should be no moldy or soft spots around the eyes.

Fresh pineapple can be frozen; peel, cube and pack it in jars or zipper

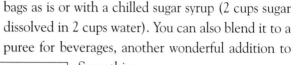

bags as is or with a chilled sugar syrup (2 cups sugar dissolved in 2 cups water). You can also blend it to a puree for beverages, another wonderful addition to Smoothies.

Remember the warnings on gelatin packages: fresh pineapple keeps gelatin from setting. It contains a tenderizing enzyme that also softens other fruits in salads; the enzyme is destroyed by cooking.

The pineapple shell itself, cut in half vertically, is an attractive container for fruit, chicken or seafood salads. Line with lettuce if necessary.

PINEAPPLE SALSA

INGREDIENTS

1 cup fresh pineapple, diced
•
2 tablespoons cilantro, chopped
•
3 tablespoons red bell pepper, diced
•
3/4 to 1 cup orange, diced
•
2 tablespoons fresh or frozen lime juice
•
1 teaspoon white sugar
•
2 teaspoons brown sugar
•
1 teaspoon vinegar
•
2 tablespoons onion, diced
•
1/2 teaspoon fresh ginger, minced
•
1 teaspoon grated orange peel
•
Salt to taste

Combine all ingredients. Serve with tortilla chips or as a refreshing accompaniment to seafood.

PINEAPPLE DAIQUIRIS

INGREDIENTS

3 cups fresh pineapple

•

1 1/2 cups light rum

•

1/3 cup sugar

•

Garnish: maraschino cherry and
mint sprig

Divide ingredients (except garnishes) in half. In blender, process each batch with 2-3 cups of ice until slushy. Garnish with mint and maraschino cherry.

SERVES 8.

MIXED FRUIT SALAD WITH CITRUS DRESSING

DRESSING INGREDIENTS

1 cup fresh orange juice

•

1/2 cup fresh or frozen lemon
(or lime) juice

•

1/2 cup dark brown sugar

•

1 teaspoon *each* lemon and orange
rind, grated

•

Dash balsamic vinegar

•

1/2 teaspoon *each* cinnamon and
nutmeg

In a straight-sided glass serving bowl, arrange layers of fresh fruit, all diced about the same size. Use whatever is available fresh and, if you are serving it right away, frozen (slightly thawed) strawberries, grapes, nectarines or bananas can be added. Try it with fresh pineapple, peaches, kiwi, strawberries, watermelon, oranges or papaya. Have at least four or five layers. Chill, and when serving, top with dressing.

144

—CHEESE—

Cheese is expensive. To save considerable money, buy the large blocks of warehouse cheeses with a variety of uses in mind. They won't go to waste. Check packages carefully to assure their freshness; any mold will show unless the cheese has a rind. It should be all the same color, too. A different color around the edges means it is drying out.

Careless treatment of packaged cheese probably contributes to its demise more than any other cause; a lot of cheese gets wasted simply because it wasn't properly wrapped. To protect cheese, once opened, remove it *entirely* from its original wrapper and rewrap tightly with plenty of plastic film. The film must be tight against the surface to do its job. Also, changing the wrap each time you use the cheese inhibits mold. So does covering it first with a vinegar-dampened paper towel. Some cooks swear by rubbing it with vegetable or olive oil to keep it from drying out.

Most cheeses freeze well, although some become crumbly when thawed. Keep in mind how you intend to use them before freezing. The crumbly ones will be fine for cooking. Roquefort and Bleu cheese, both crumbly anyway, don't have a chance to turn bad if they go right into the freezer in portion-sized containers. Your good parmesan and romano cheeses won't dry out nearly as fast in the freezer as they would in the refrigerator. I freeze the marvelous buttery Cambozola just to avoid temptation.

Feta, Gruyere, cheddar, mozzarella, Swiss and Monterey jack are cheeses I also freeze in small blocks for grating or cubes to go in sauces. If I know they are to be used in a couple of weeks, I sometimes grate them before freezing.

Even cottage, ricotta and cream cheese can be frozen; if the cheese becomes grainy, bring to room temperature and stir back to smoothness. Be sure to check the pull dates on cottage, cream cheese and ricotta, as their refrigerated life, once the cartons are opened, is over in a week or so. Once you open a cottage or ricotta cheese container, it rapidly deteriorates. Postpone this by covering the cheese surface with plastic film or storing the carton upside down in the refrigerator.

The following recipe was my mother Margaret's favorite way to serve cottage cheese. Serve this colorful salad on lettuce, in tomato shells or in green pepper rings. It lends itself to most salad garnishes and is a welcome, though often forgotten, company dish.

MOM'S COTTAGE CHEESE SALAD

My mother, Margaret Clark, loved this way to dress up boring cottage cheese.

INGREDIENTS

1 pound small curd cottage cheese, regular, low- or non-fat
•
5 or 6 green onions, sliced
•
1 medium tomato, finely chopped and drained
•
2 tablespoons green bell pepper, finely chopped
•
1 tablespoon red bell pepper, finely chopped
•
1/2 medium cucumber, finely chopped
•
1/4 cup light mayonnaise
•
Mrs. Dash seasoning
•
Salt and pepper to taste

Mix ingredients and refrigerate. As liquid from the cheese and other ingredients tends to form during refrigeration, it is best to put the cheese in a strainer or colander over a bowl until ready to serve.

SERVES 6-8.

CHEESE SAUCE

Put leftover pieces of cheeses you think would be compatible, wrapped tightly, into a zipper bag in the freezer. When the collection is sufficient, melt it together with basic white sauce. One of my recipe testers asked how to know which cheeses were "compatible." Guesswork, I told her – if you're not sure, pack them separately.

INGREDIENTS FOR ONE PINT OF SAUCE:

1 cup cheese, grated or cubed
•
2 tablespoons flour
•
2 tablespoons butter
•
1 cup milk

In a heavy saucepan, cook flour and butter together, stirring to avoid over-browning. Gradually add milk, stirring, then add cheese. You can also do this in the top of a double boiler, keeping the simmering water away from the pan holding the sauce. Otherwise it can become grainy. Freeze the thickened sauce in half-pint jars for a quick and easy dressing on broccoli, cauliflower, asparagus, etc., or for soups and casserole toppings.

When making quantity portions of cheese sauce for your ingredient supply, prepare enough extra for two casseroles. While the sauce is thickening, potatoes and macaroni can be cooking. Use one batch for scalloped potatoes, and one for the macaroni and cheese. Your sauce doesn't have to be thick; starch from the macaroni and potatoes combines to make it just right. Wrap and freeze.

—CREAM, SWEET AND SOUR—

The quart sizes of half and half and whipping cream from Sam's and Costco are a big saving over buying half-pints. So are the large containers of sour cream. Of the three varieties, only sour cream does not freeze well. Repackage sweet cream products in small jars and freeze with an inch of headroom. Use in sauces, soups and gravies as needed. For entertaining, whip cream ahead of time and spoon individual servings onto a cookie sheet. Freeze quickly, then store in zipper bags until ready to serve.

— E G G S —

Large, Grade A eggs are sold 18 or 36 to a carton at the warehouse stores, and either carton size is a saving over typical supermarket prices. They should be refrigerated, unwashed, preferably in a humidity-controlled section, or in a covered container. The quality of eggs purchased today is seldom a concern; we take it for granted they are perfect, and they usually are. It is important to carefully wash the shells when they are to be barely cooked, as with Caesar salad dressing or meringues, to prevent salmonella infections.

If your supply has been around a while, you can always test each egg by putting it in cold water. If it floats, don't use it. When my family moved to bush Alaska, "storage eggs" were all we knew, and we ate them many months old. Once in the city, fresh eggs took some getting used to! Eggs with no cracks in the shells really do last a long time; they might lose some flavor, but they won't hurt you.

When you have leftover uncooked yolks or whites, cover them with plastic film, and either will keep several days to be used only for cooking. The yolks, however, should first be covered with cold water to prevent formation of a film on top.

To freeze whole eggs, beat six eggs with 3/4 teaspoon sugar and 1/4 teaspoon salt. Spray plastic ice cube trays with oil and pour in the beaten eggs. Freeze, then release from trays and store in jars or freezer bags. Each cube equals one egg.

Use extra egg yolks in custards, maritata soup (see next page), cakes, puddings, salad dressings, scrambled egg dishes, or add them, cooked, to potato and pasta salads. The whites can be used for meringue pies and shells, soufflés and batters. Egg whites will reach greater volume if whipped at room temperature. Baker's secret: Put washed, unshelled eggs in warm water for three minutes before using in baking recipes. Makes for lighter cakes and greater volume.

Hard-boiled eggs that won't peel easily are a source of irritation, especially when you're in a hurry. Try this: Put the eggs in ice water for two minutes. Then dip them into boiling water for 20 seconds. Don't ask me why, but it works.

MARITATA SOUP

Try this showy, rich soup at your next dinner party for six or eight people.

INGREDIENTS

4 egg yolks

•

1 cup whipping cream

•

1 1/2 quarts chicken or beef broth

•

1/2 cup tiny Top Ramen noodles or broken vermicelli

•

1 stick butter

•

1 cup freshly grated parmesan or romano cheese

In a saucepan, bring broth to a boil. Add noodles, cooking until tender. Blend egg yolks, soft butter and grated cheese in a bowl, then stir in whipping cream. Add a little of the hot broth to the bowl, stirring, then return all to the saucepan, thoroughly blending. Heat, but do not boil, add salt and white pepper to taste, and pour into heated bowls.

SERVES 4-6.

SIMON & SEAFORT'S EGG MUSTARD DRESSING

Proprietors of the popular Anchorage restaurant named here dared to take this salad dressing off the menu, but they still get requests for it. Serve this dressing over crisp romaine leaves or fresh spinach.

INGREDIENTS

3 hardboiled eggs, separated into whites and yolks

•

1 1/2 teaspoons yellow mustard

•

3 tablespoons cider vinegar

•

3 tablespoons sugar

•

1/3 cup warm bacon drippings

•

4 slices bacon, cooked and minced

•

2 green onions

•

1 pound romaine leaves, broken

Chop egg whites. Mix egg yolks with mustard, vinegar and sugar until smooth. Toss romaine leaves with this mixture, then lightly mix with warm bacon drippings. Sprinkle egg whites, bacon pieces and onions over the top.

SERVES 4.

POTATO-ONION TORTILLA

This is a fine Spanish potluck dish that can be served hot or cold, is inexpensive, delicious, and easy to pack. Hope there will be leftovers to take home, but don't count on it.

INGREDIENTS

8 eggs, lightly beaten

•

3 tablespoons water

•

3 tablespoons butter

•

2 tablespoons bacon fat or cooking oil

•

6 small-to-medium potatoes, unpeeled

•

1 large onion, in strips

•

1 large red bell pepper, in strips

•

1 poblano chile, in rings

•

Salt and freshly ground pepper

•

1 1/2 cups cheddar cheese, grated

•

2 tablespoons parsley, minced

•

Parsley for garnish

Cut washed potatoes into julienne strips, cover with cold salted water and refrigerate for 30 minutes or so. Sauté bell pepper and onion in 1 tablespoon butter and set aside. Drain and dry potatoes and sprinkle with salt. In a skillet with 2 tablespoons butter and bacon fat, fry the potatoes until crisp and medium brown. Remove and drain on paper towel as they brown.

The tortilla can be cooked on the stove, but I prefer this foolproof method. Arrange the potatoes in a lightly-buttered non-stick pan, preferably a deep, slope-sided skillet. Arrange some of the onions and peppers over them. Beat eggs with the water, parsley, salt, pepper and cheese and pour half the mixture over the potatoes. Add remaining onions and peppers. Put the skillet in a larger pan with a half inch of water in it and bake in a 225-degree oven. When the eggs are set, about 30 minutes, add the remainder of eggs and cheese and bake until firm. (The eggs seem to cook more evenly done this way, in two steps.)

Remove the tortilla, let cool, and loosen edges from the pan. Put a serving plate over the skillet and flip the tortilla over onto the plate. Cut into small pie-shaped wedges and place sprigs of parsley in the center. Chill until ready to serve; reheat if desired. I often serve this with Homemade Chili Sauce.

SERVES 12.

HOMEMADE CHILI SAUCE

INGREDIENTS

6 medium tomatoes OR
2 medium tomatoes and 6 ounces tomato sauce

•

3/4 cup *each* onion and green pepper

•

1/4 cup sugar

•

2 teaspoons salt, or to taste

•

Freshly ground pepper

•

3/4 teaspoon *each* cinnamon, nutmeg, cloves

•

1/2 teaspoon allspice

•

3/4 cup white vinegar

Simmer diced tomatoes, peppers and onions over low heat for 40 minutes. Add spices and vinegar and continue cooking until sauce thickens. Test seasonings, adding a dash of Balsamic vinegar if desired. Serve with Potato-Onion Tortilla or other egg dishes.

—ICE CREAM DESSERTS—

Here is a good way to protect the flavor of ice cream, sherbet, sorbets and frozen yogurt, particularly when you buy them in large-sized containers. If they are packed in cardboard cartons, give them a new home in plastic or glass, and be sure to lay plastic film right on top of the contents to prevent freezer burn.

For easy removal, soften desserts in the microwave (on defrost setting). When entertaining, freeze scoops of these desserts on a cookie sheet covered with plastic wrap, then rewrap. This can be done a day or so ahead of time. Better still, freeze them in dessert cups or glasses set on a tray.

When ready to serve, cover the frozen dessert with a fruit puree or add fancy cookies. Or, mix some of your frozen berries with a little jam or jelly. Takes just moments away from your guests. Here is an easy chocolate sauce that keeps well refrigerated, made special by adding hazelnut liqueur or imitation hazelnut flavoring.

CHOCOLATE HAZELNUT SAUCE

INGREDIENTS

1 cup sugar
•
1 cup water
•
6 ounces unsweetened chocolate pieces
•
1 cup half-and-half cream
•
1/2 cup Frangelico liqueur

In the microwave oven, bring sugar and water to a boil, stirring to dissolve the sugar. Add chocolate pieces; stir to melt. When mixture is smooth, stir in half-and-half cream and Frangelico liqueur. Cool. Pour over ice cream.

SERVES 4-6.

PEACHY ORANGE SHERBET

You'll never be caught without a dessert in emergencies with orange sherbet and peach schnapps on hand. Surround scoops of orange sherbet or sorbet with peach schnapps for a refreshing, fat-free dessert. That's the recipe.

— M I L K —

A gallon of milk at my house can sour before it's consumed. We solved that problem with packaging that better suited our needs. Four quart-size canning jars – two for the freezer and two for the refrigerator. (Glass protects the flavor better than plastic or waxed cardboard containers.) Because Murphy's Law assures you always run out of milk at the wrong time, it is handy to have a stash in the freezer.

Milk can be defrosted in the microwave, in the refrigerator or at room temperature. If you don't want to use freezer space for milk, keep the powdered variety on hand. Another convenient form of milk, available in cases of 12 quart boxes, is the sterilized version that does not have to be refrigerated. The boxed milk keeps longer, once opened, than does fresh. It's not bad at all.

TIP: Want to save 50% of the cost of low-fat milk? Don't pay for skim, 1% or 2% milk. Seems you're just buying and hauling a lot of water home. Make your own low-fat variety. Simply dilute whole milk. A half gallon of 4% milk becomes 2% if you add an equal amount of water and divide it between two half gallon containers. Of course you also dilute the vitamin content. Add a little dry milk powder to make up for the lost milk solids.

When you have more milk than you can use right away, it is time for Plan B. Cook up a quart or two of white sauce or cheese sauce and pop it in the freezer for another day. Even slightly soured milk can be used for the sauces.

Why use canning jars? Canning jars take up less room than gallon milk jugs. Another plus: Milk keeps longer the fewer times a container is opened. A small quantity of milk in a gallon container will spoil much faster than milk stored in a smaller container with less exposed to the air.

NOTE: Those used milk cartons are great for freezing soups, stews, etc. Tear the carton away and place the contents in a large pot or microwave dish to reheat.

— YOGURT —

In addition to the 2-pound cartons of plain yogurt, both Sam's and Costco carry flats of 12 fruit-flavored yogurt varieties. Don't be afraid to use yogurt beyond the date stamped on each carton; as long as it tastes good and shows no signs of mold, it's edible. Plain yogurt can be used to replace sour cream, mayonnaise and heavy cream in many recipes.

FROZEN PEACH YOGURT

INGREDIENTS

1 cup lowfat cottage cheese
•
2 cups frozen peach puree
•
1 cup light brown sugar
•
1 tablespoon lemon juice
•
1 cup plain yogurt, regular or nonfat

Process cottage cheese in blender until smooth. Combine peach puree, sugar and lemon juice in bowl. Add yogurt and cottage cheese, mixing well. Turn into ice cube trays and freeze. Remove from freezer and beat to break up ice crystals. Refreeze and remove shortly before serving to soften.

SERVES 4.

BAKERY ITEMS

— BREAD —

Warehouse bread usually comes two-loaves-to-a-package. That may seem like a lot of bread for your needs. It could be, unless you consider the product's potential as an ingredient for a multitude of dishes.

Don't store bread in the refrigerator; it will quickly dry out. An exception is refrigerating it in a Tupperware-type container with the air removed. That extra loaf should go right to the freezer, but not as is. In its loose package, ice crystals will light on each available surface. Try this: Force the air out and wrap the loaf tightly with plastic film before putting it in another container or zipper bag.

There are *at least* five good reasons not to waste stale bread – garlic croutons, bread pudding, poultry stuffing, French toast and seasoned bread crumbs.

FRENCH TOAST

In a flat bowl beat 3 or 4 eggs lightly and add 1/2 teaspoon each salt and vanilla and a cup of milk. Dip eight slices of bread in the mixture, turning each over. Brown the slices in a buttered skillet or on a griddle and top with a cinnamon-sugar mixture or maple syrup. A great stand-in for pancakes, and faster to do. You can freeze the browned slices if you like, and warm them up in the toaster.

GARLIC CROUTONS

The best croutons are made from French bread, but we're not picky. You can routinely cube almost any non-sweet leftover bread and toss it in the freezer until you have enough for a marathon crouton-making session. (A good time for this is when you're stuck in the kitchen doing something else.)

Spread the frozen cubes on a cookie sheet and toast them lightly in the oven at 350 to 450 degrees. Sauté butter (or a mixture of butter and olive oil), some salt and garlic in a skillet and drizzle it over the bread cubes, baking and turning a few more minutes until they are a nice light brown color. Freeze or store in the refrigerator in a covered jar. They're ready for Caesar and other salads, hot and cold soups and casseroles.

MEXICAN CORNBREAD

Also called Mexican spoon bread, custard or pudding, this recipe is dense and moist. No extra butter is needed which makes it convenient for buffets. I bake this in miniature or regular muffin tins (fewer crumbs than skillet cornbread). The frozen muffins can be popped into the microwave and heated right in the freezer bag.

INGREDIENTS

1 1/2 sticks butter

•

1/2 cup sugar

•

4 eggs

•

1 cup green chiles, chopped

•

1 jalapeño pepper, minced

•

2 cups cream-style corn

•

1 cup grated sharp cheddar

•

1 cup grated jack cheese

•

1 1/2 cups each flour and yellow cornmeal

•

4 teaspoons baking powder

•

1/2 teaspoon each salt and chili powder

•

Optional: 2 tablespoons roasted red pepper, chopped, and 2 tablespoons onion, minced

Cream butter and sugar. Add eggs, one by one, mixing after each. Add chiles, corn, cheeses and optional ingredients. Mix dry ingredients and add all at once. Grease and flour muffin tins or cornstick pans and fill sections three-quarters full. Bake in 350-degree oven. Check for doneness after 45 minutes and bake 10-15 minutes more if needed.

MAKES 12 LARGE OR 24 MINIATURE MUFFINS.

OLD-FASHIONED BREAD PUDDING WITH LEMON SAUCE

Another reason to hoard leftover bread is for luscious pudding. Used this way, many kinds of bread mixed together contribute unique flavors to this often-neglected dish. Served warm with rum sauce or my favorite, an intensely flavored lemon sauce, bread pudding is a delightful change of pace in the dessert department. This recipe makes enough for two casseroles, each serving eight.

INGREDIENTS

8-12 cups of bread cubes, with or without crusts
•
6 eggs, slightly beaten
•
6 cups milk, or milk and part orange juice, to cover bread
•
1 cup white, light or dark brown sugar
•
1 cup plumped raisins
•
Grated rind of 2 lemons, yellow part only
•
Cinnamon, nutmeg, cloves, allspice, to taste
•
Chopped nuts, optional
•
1/2 cup applesauce or apple butter, optional

LEMON SAUCE INGREDIENTS

3 tablespoons lemon juice
•
Grated rind of one lemon
•
1/4 cup butter
•
1 cup sugar
•
3 eggs, slightly beaten

Spread bread cubes in buttered baking dishes from which you can serve. Mix remaining ingredients and pour over bread. Let sit a few minutes to absorb. Optional ingredients should be added at this point. If you have too much liquid, add more bread – or vice versa. Set the baking dish in a larger container holding about 1/2 inch of water. Cover loosely with foil to prevent over-browning, but remove foil during last 10 minutes of baking. Bake about an hour in a 350-degree oven.

Note: Apple butter and applesauce are already seasoned; that's why I specify no amount for the spices; let taste be your guide. Serve with lemon sauce.

Put lemon juice in a saucepan with the grated lemon rind and butter. Cook two minutes. Add sugar and eggs. Cook and stir over low heat until thick. This is enough for one casserole.

SERVES 8-10.

MARIANO'S POULTRY STUFFING

The best turkey stuffing I ever tasted was at a mercury mine in Red Devil, Alaska, prepared by a Basque cook named Mariano Juan Corino. Mariano had invited us for Thanksgiving dinner, and we flew down on the mail plane. Someday, he said, he would take my sister and me to his home in Spain but, alas, he returned there without us.

We have his roast turkey and dressing to remember him by, at least. The stuffing was practically all cornbread, celery, onions, and seasonings. It is difficult to put too much celery and onions in poultry stuffing, so don't worry about exact measurements. A secret I share with people who ask is, add the celery and onions raw, without sautéing first, as some cookbooks advise. Gives the stuffing a more intense flavor and texture.

This recipe makes about 12 cups. If it doesn't fit inside both ends of your chicken or turkey, bake it in a separate dish until lightly browned.

INGREDIENTS

1 1/2 cups *each* chopped celery and chopped onion, or more

•

6 cups stale bread cubes from your freezer supply

•

3 cups cornbread, crumbled

•

1 cup cooked sausage meat, drained (optional)

•

1 cup chopped mushrooms (optional)

•

2 eggs, lightly beaten

•

1/2 cup chopped parsley

•

3/4 cup soft butter

•

Salt and freshly ground pepper to taste

•

1/2 to 1 teaspoon *each* sage, rosemary, thyme and nutmeg

•

Chicken broth, made with giblets, to moisten

Combine the ingredients up to the chicken broth, tossing well to blend the flavors. Let sit a while, then moisten the stuffing with chicken broth. Chop some of the giblets and add them, too, if you like. Correct seasonings and stuff the bird just before roasting.

SERVES 10-12

SEASONED BREADCRUMBS

For tasty breadcrumbs, whirl your baked, garlic-seasoned bread cubes in the blender or food processor. Or, make them from plain bread that is dry or lightly toasted. For Italian-seasoned crumbs add – well, Italian seasoning.

Breadcrumbs, sautéed in a skillet with a tablespoon of butter per cup of crumbs, are excellent for thickening soups, a topping for casseroles, or sprinkled over vegetables. Use them also for breading meats and seafood. Store as you would croutons.

— PIE CRUSTS —

The triple package of Pillsbury All-ready Piecrusts, two in each box, is so convenient that it hardly makes sense to mess up the kitchen making piecrusts. Because each crust is cellophane-wrapped, the keeping quality in the refrigerator or freezer makes this a worthwhile purchase. Use frozen crusts within three months.

If you need that piecrust now, it can be thawed in the microwave in seconds. Before your friends arrive rub some flour on your face, leave a rolling pin* on the counter, and your visitors will never know all you did was unroll the crust and brush it with egg yolk for that homemade touch. "Of course I baked a pie when I heard you might drop in!"

*Rolling pin: an ancient cylindrical utensil used for flattening cave-made pastry.

Think beyond desserts for piecrust uses – beef or chicken pot pies, quiche, stews, filled appetizers.

— PIES, CAKES, COOKIES AND MUFFINS —

The superb, reasonably priced pastries from the warehouse bakeries are a justifiable temptation. They truly are as good as they look. If you're watching calories, though, it doesn't help to have a huge chocolate raspberry torte, cherry pie or carrot cake making eyes at you from the kitchen counter.

Solve that problem in a hurry by partially freezing, then cutting them into neat serving-size slices, and wrapping each slice thoroughly in plastic wrap. The wrapped slices go into a cookie tin or other container to provide additional protection from freezer wrath. I usually have slices of several cakes on hand for company – they look great decked out on a fancy cake platter, besides providing variety. Same goes for those delectable warehouse bakery cookies and giant muffins. Kept this way, you should find them even more economical.

When serving the warehouse muffins and bar cookies, it's nice to offer several varieties, arranging them in slices rather than serving whole. Besides being quite attractive on the serving platter, the slices offer diners a chance to taste more than one. They go farther served this way, too. Incidentally, if your baked goods are left at room temperature for any length of time, be sure to keep them covered to preserve freshness.

Should cakes and muffins begin to dry out, all is not lost. Cut them in chunks, pour a fruity liqueur over, and you have another excellent dessert, with or without ice cream. You can also moisten them with this simple syrup:

→

STALE CAKE SAVER

INGREDIENTS

1 cup orange or pineapple juice

•

1/2 cup sugar

•

2 tablespoons rum or fruit brandy

Combine sugar and juice in a saucepan. Cook until sugar dissolves. Cool and add rum or brandy.

—PIZZA SHELLS—

"Let's have pizza tonight" is a more plausible suggestion when you don't have to make the shells from scratch, head for the pizza parlor, wait for a delivery, or settle for a commercial brand. You are minutes away from your own pizza specialty with either the warehouse Boboli cheese-baked shells or the frozen plain ones individually shrink-wrapped in a triple-pack.

Then there are the delectable Italian foccacia breads which you can eat as is or with minimal toppings. Compare the warehouse prices with what you usually pay for a pizza "fix," and you may be in for a big surprise.

INSTANT GOURMET PIZZA

Your ingredient arsenal will hold everything you need to make the best pizza around.
Start with a pizza shell and add your choice of toppings.

Anchovy fillets
Artichoke hearts
Basil and pine nut pesto
Basil, parsley and oregano
Canadian bacon
Chicken
Cilantro pesto
Cream, whipping
Extra-virgin olive oil
Garlic, plain, roasted
Gorgonzola cheese
Green chiles
Green, yellow and red peppers
Ground beef and onions
Herbs and spices

Italian sausage
Mozzarella cheese
Mushrooms
Mussels
Olives, black, green
Onions, white, red, green
Parmesan cheese
Romano cheese
Pepperoni, sliced
Pine nuts
Pineapple chunks
Pizza sauce (from #10 can)
Scallops
Shrimp
Sun-dried tomatoes

— T O R T I L L A S —

Both corn and flour tortillas are available at Sam's and Costco. Wrapped tightly and refrigerated, the corn tortillas will last a few days, the flour ones much longer. Better to freeze if not quickly used.

If you haven't tried them, Reser's oversized spinach, basil pesto and tomato-seasoned flour tortillas offer a satisfying and popular holder for all kinds of cooked bean, fresh veggie, meat or combination fillings. I've also purchased a combination of cheese, jalapeño and salsa-flavored wraps.The packages contain ten of each flavor, separately wrapped. The tortillas freeze nicely, and with your stockpile of prepared ingredients, it takes just minutes to put a meal together.

When using flour tortillas this way, toast them lightly in a dry skillet, folding as ingredients are inserted. This toasting imparts a better flavor and texture, but take care not to burn them. They are also excellent in casseroles, tostadas, or cut into quarters and deep-fried for use as chips. Taco salad, served in a deep-fried tortilla "bowl," is an attractive, nourishing lunch or supper dish.

To warm a stack of flour or corn tortillas, wrap them in a damp towel and microwave on low or medium power for about one minute. You can also use a warm conventional oven or steam them, wrapped, over a pot of hot water. Keep tortillas warm in a covered container.

T O R T I L L A   R O L L U P   A P P E T I Z E R

For an easy appetizer, cut flour tortillas in half (untoasted), spread with a seasoned bean or spicy cream-cheese based filling and roll them up. After chilling a while, seam side down, cut the rolls every inch or so and arrange, cut side up, on serving platter with some decorative greens.

Seafood, chicken, seasoned pork, avocado blends, and almost any of your favorite dips or spreads are suitable for this appetizer. You do need a binder to hold the tortilla together, which cream cheese does very well.

ZENAIDA'S CALDO DE PANELA (CHEESE AND TORTILLA SOUP)

Zenaida Quijada, one of the excellent cooks at Alamos, Sonora's elegant new spa hotel, Casa de los Santos, prepares this simple soup for friends. It uses a local cheese, called panela, but Monterey jack is a good substitute.

INGREDIENTS

2 tomatoes, diced

•

1/2 cup onions, diced

•

4 cloves garlic, minced

•

2 Anaheim or poblano chiles, roasted and peeled

•

1/2 pound Mexican panela cheese or Monterey Jack, 3/4" cubes

•

8 corn tortillas, quartered

•

3 tablespoons vegetable oil

•

1 cup milk

•

4 cups water

•

Salt and pepper to taste

Fry tortilla quarters in vegetable oil until crisp. In a skillet, sauté tomatoes, onions, garlic and chiles. Season with salt and pepper. Pour vegetables into a saucepan and add water. Bring to boil and simmer 20 minutes. Add cheese, milk and tortillas and simmer 5 more minutes. Cheese will not be melted. Serve with limes and chopped cilantro for true Mexican flavor.

SERVES 6.

DESSERT TOSTADA

Deep-fried flour tortilla "baskets," served in restaurants to hold combinations of meat, beans, lettuce, tomatoes, sour cream, etc., are also excellent for presenting luscious desserts. They can be prepared in advance and filled just before serving.

A handy tool for frying the tortillas, a tortilla basket maker, simplifies their preparation. You can also press the tortillas into a large strainer to form the basket. Deep-fry them in hot oil (375 degrees) until light brown; then quickly turn out upside down on paper towels.

Fill plain flour tortillas with flan, chocolate mousse, fruit combinations or cake and ice cream.

MISCELLANEOUS

—CANNED GOODS—

A question many warehouse club members ask concerns the large six-pound-plus cans of sauces, vegetables and fruits. The question is: "Once the can is opened, can I freeze the rest of the contents?"

The answer is: "Yes, but only if you have abundant freezer space." My first purchase of this nature was pizza sauce. Sauces freeze well, so my plan was to freeze the leftover sauce in small jars holding just enough for one large pizza. The experiment was successful, and the savings considerable. It took more than a year to use up the pizza sauce, but there was no deterioration in the product that I could detect.

Would it have been more economical to use that space for a higher-value frozen product? Yes, but cost isn't the only consideration. The deciding factor for me concerned whether keeping the pizza sauce on hand contributed to my ability to do ingredient cooking and have pizza on a moment's notice.

Canned artichoke hearts, black olives, roasted red peppers, whole and diced green chiles, tomato puree, crushed tomatoes, mushrooms, jalapeno peppers, olive oil, pineapple tidbits, and sliced beets are the institutional-sized items that first come to mind. I'm sure there are more and, no question about it, you can save considerable money buying in this quantity.

How About Canning? My friend Carol, who cooks just for her husband and herself in Alamos, buys the big cans and repackages what she doesn't use right away. She, like many of the *gringos* who live here, brings back products from the "states" that aren't available in Sonora. They go in sterilized jars which then go into a pressure cooker or boiling water bath. I don't do this because I get nervous about germs that have names like *clostridium botulinum*. Of course, if you know all about canning and the necessary precautions, go for it.

—COFFEE AND TEA—

COFFEE. The whole coffee bean varieties, even espresso, available from the warehouse stores are excellent buys, even if it takes a long time to use them up. Stored in an airtight jar in the freezer, they are good for a year. Keeping air away from the coffee beans is critical; nothing does it better than the Food Saver vacuum sealer. For coffee connoisseurs who can't vacuum pack their coffee, but are willing to go the extra mile to maintain its flavor, read on.

Alaska's Kaladi Brothers Coffee Company instructs customers in great detail about the three basic components affecting coffee flavor – body, acidity and aroma. In less detail, the explanation means "together CO_2 and aroma volatiles can be referred to as gasses. The gasses are the smell of coffee. And when the gasses go away, the flavor goes with it. The gas acts as a barrier from oxygen – the enemy of coffee – that stales the coffee."

Kaladi Company further explains: "Gasses expand at higher temperatures and contract at lower temperatures. Thus, lowering the temperature of these gasses slows their rate of dissipation. At temperatures below freezing the gasses don't expand at all. So put your coffee in the freezer to keep it fresh!"

Grind coffee just before you use it for best flavor. For company, you can brew the coffee an hour or two before guests arrive and keep it hot in a preheated insulated carafe, but under no circumstances can you leave it on a burner without ruining it.

Iced coffee is popular in Alamos, and friends hate to waste a drop of their stateside warehouse brands. Fresh cold coffee is poured into ice cube trays and frozen. Instead of ice, the coffee cubes are put in glasses with additional cold coffee poured over. No weak coffee for this crowd!

Keep a small jar of instant coffee on hand in case you make a pot that is too weak. A tablespoon of instant added to the pot will repair the damage.

If the water in your area has too much chlorine or certain minerals in it, you can bet the coffee will be affected. Bottled water can solve that problem.

TEA. The same comments about water apply to tea-making.

After leaving Kentucky for Alaska, I never lost the habit of drinking iced tea. On a cold winter day, there I am, hands around an ice-cold glass while everyone else sucks up hot coffee. One problem with this habit, though, is I hate to unwrap tea bags. So I was one happy person when Sam's Club began carrying the cartons of gallon-sized tea bags. Now I make a pitcher in the morning without grumbling.

Once the package is opened, store tea bags in a covered jar or zipper bag in a cool, dark place. Two questions I was asked recently: What to do about cloudy tea? Pour in some boiling water. Don't refrigerate tea until it cools or it will become cloudy. How do you make sun tea? Fill a container with water, put in the teabags and let it sit in the sun, covered to keep the bugs out, for four or five hours. Make some tea both ways and see if people can tell the difference.

—COOKING AND SALAD OILS—

Once, years ago, I threw out a gallon jug of vegetable oil that turned rancid. It had been stored in a hot garage in Kentucky. For a long time after that I bought oil only in much smaller sizes. Now I'm back to the larger sizes but am much more careful about where and how it is stored.

If you use an opened container within a year, cool, dark room temperature storage is adequate. However, most solid and liquid oils last much longer refrigerated. Because refrigerator space is at a premium,

I pour some of the oil into a large, tall container and stash it in one of those inaccessible refrigerator spaces, out of the way. The rest goes in a pretty corked bottle on the counter.

Ah, the amazing variety of marvelous, fruity extra-virgin olive oils that we get to choose from today. Remember when Napoleon was the only brand? Try the extra-virgin olive oils carried by the warehouses, some in lovely decorative bottles.

—GINGER—

This isn't a warehouse food item, but you need to have it on hand because there's no suitable substitute. I have wasted more fresh ginger than you can imagine and, invariably, when I am finally ready to use some, there it is decaying in its grave, the vegetable bin. There are solutions:

(1) Store small pieces of ginger in Madeira wine, refrigerated, in a covered jar for several months,

(2) Grate the ginger and freeze it in a spice jar for a month or so; or

(3) Freeze whole pieces of ginger wrapped tightly with plastic film in a zipper bag. This last option will keep your ginger indefinitely. If its flavor diminishes, you will know when "indefinitely" ends.

GINGER-SOY DRESSING

INGREDIENTS

1/2 cup salad oil
•
1/4 to 1/3 cup sugar
•
3 tablespoons catsup
•
3 tablespoons cider vinegar
•
2 tablespoons Worcestershire sauce
•
1/2 tablespoon grated ginger
•
1/3 cup soy sauce

Blend ingredients in a jar and serve over oriental chicken or cabbage salads.

LEMON-GINGER SYRUP

This simple but delightful syrup was wonderful over vanilla ice cream, a delicate flavor following a shrimp curry dinner I attended recently. Try it over fresh fruit, my hostess suggested. She doubled this recipe for her twelve guests.

INGREDIENTS

1 piece fresh ginger, 3 inches x 1 1/2 inches
•
1 large lemon
•
1/2 cup sugar
•
1 1/2 cups water
•
1/4 cup fresh mint leaves

Peel lemon from top to bottom with a sharp knife or peeler (yellow skin only) in eight equal strips. Cut part of the strips into tiny slivers, leaving the remainder their full length. Mince part of the ginger and slice the remainder thinly. Put all ingredients in a small pan and bring to a boil, stirring. Simmer uncovered about 15 minutes or until syrup is reduced to one cup. Strain, leaving just the syrup, and refrigerate up to a week.

— HERBS AND SPICES —

SPICES AND SEASONING BLENDS. Although the large restaurant-sized jars of spices are a great bargain, keep in mind that spices can deteriorate in a matter of months after opening. If you can't bear to toss them when they no longer smell fresh and powerful, you're better off sharing these items with a shopping mate or freezing part of your supply. Yes, freezing. The same goes for those great seasoning blends. Your Lemon Pepper, Steak Seasoning, Mrs. Dash, Taco, Cajun and Spaghetti Sauce Seasoning will be just fine in the freezer for months and months.

Another trick for making your spices last longer involves putting some in a small spice jar for frequent use and repacking the remainder in a jar that barely holds the contents so that no air gets to it. Or, use the Food Saver to remove the air. This may seem like a lot of trouble, but once you start keeping the right containers handy for such purposes, it won't be. Ounce for ounce, few food items cost more than spices and seasoning blends, so you might as well do what you can to extend their useful life.

Those spices that have been on the shelf too long can be revived by toasting them lightly in a skillet, heating them in the microwave, and crumbling them with your fingers before adding to recipes. I now make it a habit to toast spices whether they are old or not. I also like mixing all the spices called for in a recipe together with a mortar and pestle to bring out the flavor.

FRESH HERBS. Until some smart entrepreneurs got the idea for providing it, supermarkets seldom stocked dependable supplies of fresh herbs. Today, in many areas they are grown locally, assuring availability and excellent quality. Almost any food tastes better with the addition of fresh rather than dried herbs. Usually available are basil, cilantro, dill, oregano, mint, tarragon, Italian and curly parsley, rosemary, sage and thyme.

Fresh herbs keep best wrapped in a damp paper towel, then in a zipper bag to be refrigerated. Bunches of parsley or cilantro do well refrigerated with their feet in water and a plastic bag tied over the top of the container. Change the water daily.

Freezing Herbs. There is a way to do it that preserves the flavor pretty well. Snip or pull the leaves off and pile them loosely into a paper cup or muffin tin. Cover with cold water and freeze, then repackage. Thaw in a colander and use right away. Basil, tarragon, mint and dill taste better frozen than dried.

See the Butter listing for Herb Butter suggestions.

Drying Herbs. At my friend Linda's house recently, I saw her herb-drying project which involved window screens stacked all over the place with the leaves of ten different herbs neatly spread on top. She warned me not to walk fast or the breeze might blow them from the screen.

Never shy about offering advice, I asked why she didn't dry them in the microwave oven. Her mouth dropped open as though I had suggested she store jars upside down in the refrigerator or something. It turned out she had never heard of drying herbs that way. Just like storing onions in panty hose – we think everyone *knows* these things.

Remove the glass tray from the microwave oven and cover it with paper towels. Arrange the herbs in a single layer on the towel and zap them on *high* for a minute or so. Repeat if necessary, just keep watching so they don't burn. Like a miracle, they will dry right before your eyes.

—NUTS—

Pecans, walnuts, peanuts, pine nuts, cashews, pistachios, almonds – adding these tasty delicacies to meats, salads, casseroles and desserts imparts unique texture and flavor. The two-pound bags can go rancid because of their fat content unless you use them within a few months.

Don't take a chance – freeze your nut supply in airtight containers and they'll keep their flavor indefinitely. It is worth using the freezer space because nuts are expensive, and there is quite a saving buying them from the warehouse stores. I've used them more than a year old stored this way, always toasting them first. Refrigerated, they should keep up to four months, depending upon how fresh they were when purchased.

Nut flavors and crunchiness are enhanced by toasting them in the oven at 300-350 degrees for 5-7 minutes or in a skillet with a little butter. You do have to pay attention as nuts burn easily,

especially pine nuts. You can accomplish the same thing by laying them out on a paper towel in the microwave for several minutes.

If you need to remove the skins from almonds or hazelnuts, wrap them in a dish towel immediately after removing them from the oven. Roll them around in the towel after a few minutes and the skins will loosen.

Before I learned this trick, I used to have trouble with chopped nuts sinking in bread and cake batters: Toss them with flour first or toast them as described previously. Both methods work fine. You can also grind the nuts and substitute them for a small amount of the flour in baked goods. Gives you the flavor, but not the crunch.

A trendy and delicious use for ground nuts is to coat fish filets with them before baking or frying. Use as you would bread or cracker crumbs.

SPICED NUTS

INGREDIENTS

2 tablespoons butter

•

1 tablespoon olive oil

•

Splash of Tabasco Sauce

•

1 tablespoon Worcestershire Sauce

•

1 teaspoon *each* salt and cumin

•

1/2 teaspoon paprika

•

1 garlic clove

•

2 cups walnut or pecan halves

Put all but the nuts and salt in a saucepan and heat to blend. Add the nuts, stirring into seasonings. Sprinkle nuts on a cookie sheet and place in a 325-degree oven for 15 minutes. Watch to prevent burning. Toss with salt. A nice appetizer.

LEMON PECANS

INGREDIENTS

2 cups pecans

•

1 teaspoon salt

•

1 cup sugar

•

Grated peel of four lemons, yellow
only

•

1/2 teaspoon *each* nutmeg and
cinnamon

•

2 teaspoons fresh lemon juice

•

2 egg whites

This recipe takes a little more time than the previous one, but you'll like it. Mix in a bowl the salt, sugar, lemon peel and spices. In another bowl mix the egg whites and lemon juice with a wire whisk until foamy. Add the pecans, stirring to coat. Shake the nuts a few at a time in a strainer to remove excess lemon-egg mixture. Spread the coated nuts on a foil-covered cookie sheet. Sprinkle with sugar-spice mixture, and then mix with hands to thoroughly coat. Bake at 250 degrees about 40 minutes, checking frequently to prevent over-browning.

CINDY'S ORIENTAL WALNUTS

My friend Cindy grows walnuts in California and is glad to share this recipe.

INGREDIENTS

2 cups walnut halves

•

2 tablespoons soy sauce

•

2 tablespoons Dijon mustard

•

1 tablespoon vegetable oil

•

1 tablespoon *each* honey and ground
ginger

•

3/4 teaspoon crushed rosemary

•

1/2 teaspoon garlic salt

•

Sesame seeds

Combine soy, mustard, oil and spices in a bowl. Mix in the walnuts. Lift the nuts out with a slotted spoon, and then toss with sesame seeds. Spread on a foil-covered cookie sheet and bake at 250 about 40 minutes. Store in airtight container.

PINE NUTS: The two-pound bags of pine nuts at the warehouse stores are an enormous saving over those found in the grocery stores. In Seattle it was not unusual to pay $14 a pound for them, and in Anchorage even more. I was stunned the first time I paid less than $5 for the two-pound package at Costco. This price jumps dramatically, however, if the pine nut crop is limited.

A few pine nuts lightly toasted in butter – not too many, because they are a high-fat item – are a unique and wonderful addition to salads, meats, desserts, and sprinkled over vegetables. Homemade pesto, prepared for steamed vegetables or pasta, makes memorable dishes. If you prefer the milder flavor of parmesan in your pesto, use that instead of the romano cheese in the following recipe.

You can also make pesto with cilantro instead of basil, but for company, keep in mind that people tend to either love or hate this pungent member of the parsley family.

BASIL PINE NUT PESTO

INGREDIENTS

6 cups basil, stemmed

•

1 1/2 cups pine nuts

•

3/4 cup Bertolli olive oil

•

1 1/2 cups Pecorino romano cheese, freshly grated

•

1/2 cup butter (preferably unsalted)

•

3 garlic cloves, mashed

•

Salt to taste

Whirl the ingredients in the blender until finely pureed. Freeze in small portions or store in refrigerator for a few weeks.

PINE NUT SALAD DRESSING

INGREDIENTS

1 cup pine nuts, toasted
•
1/2 cup extra virgin olive oil
•
3 tablespoons rice wine vinegar
•
3 tablespoons tarragon vinegar
•
1 scant teaspoon lemon peel, grated
•
Salt and freshly ground pepper
•
1/2 teaspoon Mrs. Dash seasoning

Blend ingredients and refrigerate. Serve over spinach or any mixed salad greens.

SHRIMP AND PINE NUT SALAD

INGREDIENTS

1 cup tiny shrimp, fresh, frozen or canned
•
1 cup roasted red bell peppers, chopped
•
3 cups fresh mushrooms, sliced
•
1 1/2 cups pitted black olives, sliced
•
1 cup pimiento or garlic-stuffed green olives
•
1 cup toasted pine nuts
•
1 cup chopped celery
•
1 16-ounce bottle Kraft Zesty Italian salad dressing

Mix ingredients and marinate in Zesty Italian salad dressing overnight. To serve, pour off the dressing and arrange shrimp-vegetable mixture on individual plates lined with lettuce leaves. Garnish with chopped egg yolks, parsley or more chopped red pepper.

SERVES 4.

—VINEGAR—

Gallon jugs of vinegar can be put to good use to save money even if you cook just for yourself. To verify this, buy a 12-ounce bottle of red or white wine vinegar. Then compare its taste and cost with wine vinegar you make. It is so simple – makes me wonder why more people don't experiment with homemade versions. With decorative corked bottles so inexpensive these days, your signature wine vinegar makes an excellent gift.

WINE VINEGAR

INGREDIENTS

2 quarts white cider vinegar
•
2 quarts dry white wine
•
4 tablespoons dried tarragon
•
2 tablespoons whole black pepper
•
1 teaspoon whole cloves
•
6 large bay leaves
•
1 tablespoon grated lemon peel

Break bay leaves into pieces and lightly crush tarragon, pepper and cloves with a mortar and pestle to release their flavors. Put all ingredients in a stainless steel or enameled pan, bring to boiling and simmer for 30 minutes. When cool, strain through a paper coffee filter or fine mesh strainer. It can be used immediately. For red wine vinegar, substitute red wine in this recipe.

HERB VINEGAR

To make herb vinegar, heat your wine vinegar and immerse fresh herbs such as rosemary, tarragon, thyme, chervil, basil, parsley in various combinations and let them steep, covered, for two weeks in the refrigerator. Then strain the vinegar and pour into sterile corked bottles. It will keep, refrigerated, for about six months.

VINEGAR AND OIL DRESSING

Use one part wine vinegar to two parts extra virgin olive oil to make your own salad dressing. For a fruity dressing, add fresh raspberries, mint and a little honey, or toss in some fresh herbs and garlic. You will enjoy this much more than commercial varieties.

PART III:

Buying Big:
How to
Make it Last

CANNING JARS, BOTTLES

Pick up some wide-mouth quart, pint and half-pint Mason or Kerr jars with matching lids. They work well for storing staples on the shelf, refrigerated items, and food prepared for the freezer. There are definite advantages to being able to see what is in the container.

Dry foods packed in jars (any kind) remain fresh longer than in their original opened boxes or bags. For long-term storage, you can easily remove the air from canning jars with the Food Saver air extraction system. Flour, rice, pasta and beans particularly benefit from the extra protection. (This step isn't necessary for foods you use regularly.)

You can also use recycled commercial jars with their own lids for freezing, particularly the half-gallon and gallon sizes (glass or plastic) which are excellent for soup bases, browned meat, pasta sauce, chili, cooked dried beans, etc. Do keep in mind, however, that it is best to freeze in meal-sized portions.

People tell me they didn't know food could be frozen in glass. It can, as long as you leave room for the contents to expand *and* thaw their contents gradually. (You do not want to defrost the jar of pasta sauce on "high" in the microwave.) Tempered glass containers, especially made for freezing, also can be purchased.

Keep a dozen or so of the squat, 16-ounce or similar-sized glass drink bottles on hand for storing fruit and vegetable purees. I bought a case of Starbuck's Frappuccino without even knowing whether I liked the coffee product – solely for the bottles. They look like miniature old-fashioned milk bottles. These wide-mouth containers wash easily, have resealable lids, fit nicely in freezer doors, and are great for carrying Smoothies to work.

Hint: With the lids on tight, store fresh, frozen or refrigerated foods in jars *upside down*. People who see these jars might whisper that you're not the sharpest knife in the drawer, but your food will last longer than theirs. This method really does keep air off the surface of your food. Try it with jellies, relishes, olives, mayonnaise, sauces, artichokes, etc.

FOOD SAVER VACUUM-SEAL SYSTEM

People who use the Food Saver Vacuum-Seal System (available at the warehouses with an instructional video) and its rolls of plastic bags, canisters and air extractors for canning jars, swear by this system. Alaska hunters and fishermen who pride themselves on the quality of their catch, are at the top of this list. Professional guides and outfitters say they rely on vacuum-sealed provisions because they keep longer. My neighbors, a retired couple, use theirs to prepare and freeze favorite dishes in individual microwaveable portions. (The Food Saver bags can go from freezer to microwave and to the dishwasher for re-use.)

Shrink-wrapping truly extends the life of almost any frozen or dry product. The manufacturer says foods keep three to five times longer than foods stored in regular zipper bags. But once you open a package, the Food Saver equipment must be used to reseal it. If your equipment and supplies are easily accessible, chances are you will make better use of the vacuum-sealing approach to food preservation.

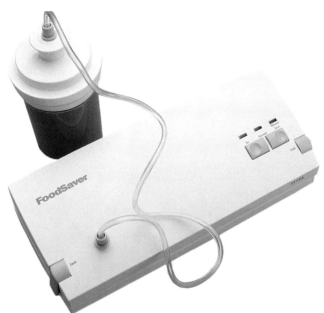

MOLDED PLASTIC CONTAINERS

Plastic storage containers of all sizes and shapes are extremely useful for storing food in the pantry, refrigerator and freezer. They are microwaveable and dishwasher safe. You can buy complete sets quite inexpensively at the warehouse stores.

Fresh milk can be poured from unwieldy gallon bottles into tall containers with handles to gain shelf space in the refrigerator. Milk can also be frozen in them. Ice cream products keep better in plastic than in cardboard, and covering the product's surface with plastic film keeps ice crystals from forming.

MILK CARTONS

"Recycled" pint, quart and half-gallon waxed milk or juice cartons are the most inexpensive freezer container for any number of foods. If the carton is not filled, cover the food surface with plastic film or waxed paper and force out the air before sealing. Another advantage to freezing in cartons is that you can separate the carton from the frozen food it contains and thaw it more quickly.

—FOOD STORAGE OPTIONS—

THE KITCHEN

Before your first buying trip, tour the kitchen to find more storage space. Move seldom-used utensils to a garage or pantry shelf. You have to find a home for your ingredient cooking supplies. Open every cabinet and drawer, and you will be amazed at the space available. In my kitchen, I found large vertical areas of wasted space in drawers, cabinets, the pantry, and even in the refrigerator.

A tall closet near the kitchen contained all sorts of household necessities, from light bulbs to cookbooks to barbecue tools, but the shelves had 15 inches of space between them, with less than half used. The bottom shelf was two feet from the floor, practically useless.

To the rescue – the sturdy pullout drawers manufactured by Sterilite and Tupperware. Not boxes with lids mind you, but self-contained covered drawers. Available in several sizes and colors from superstores like Fred Meyer, Target, Wal-Mart and K-Mart, they also stack neatly on each other. Plus, when you pull one drawer out, the others stay in place. After taking careful measurements and spending nearly $100 on the drawers (buy them on sale), I was able to double – and in one case triple – my available storage space.

SOMEWHERE ELSE

Do you have a garage, closet, laundry room or basement for storing quantity purchases such as large bags of pet food, cases of paper products and food staples? If you could use more shelf space, installing it is a fun-to-do (well, in some circles) Saturday project that will reward you with ample room at convenient heights.

The warehouse stores carry sturdy, inexpensive shelving units, both metal and plastic, and some have rollers for moving them around. Like the plastic storage drawers, you can take these units with you when you move.

Don't store food on a basement or garage floor; too many things can happen to it there. Protect and maintain its integrity by storing everything on shelves in airtight or covered containers, with legible labels. But keep it cool. Use lower shelves if the space is warm. You may also find it convenient to store most of an item, say, flour, in a large airtight plastic box, and part of it in a smaller, more accessible container in the kitchen.

Alaska friends who live in the bush generally have small living quarters, many in log cabins with little built-in storage space. "Going to town" (which usually involves a plane trip), and shopping the warehouses is a big event, and finding places to store their supplies a challenge. Staples go under the coffee table, in closets, under beds, behind sofas, in bathroom cabinets, etc. When I hear people say they don't have room for large-quantity purchases, it makes me wonder if they've given it much creative thought.

THE REFRIGERATOR

My dream refrigerator would be completely open down the middle, from the top to the produce bins. The shelves would slide out, and all the contents would be visible. There would always be enough room on each shelf for similar-sized items. My idea of fun is not crawling on the floor to get something out of a low refrigerator shelf, or trying to rearrange the contents to squeeze in one more item. Drastic measures are called for if you also don't own the perfect refrigerator.

Take the time to do this: Move everything from the refrigerator to the kitchen counters and group each item by size. Then readjust the shelves accordingly. If top-shelf space is limited, see what foods or beverages can be repackaged. Gallon milk and juice jugs, for instance, consume way too much room, plus you can't stack anything on them. Instead, pour the milk or juice into tall, skinny covered containers, preferably clear glass, so you can identify the contents. Look at what you can repackage into smaller containers (that half-gallon jar with four pickles in it, for instance).

To gain more room in my crowded refrigerator, I added an extra plastic drawer for fruit, one for cheese, and a large slide-out open container for small jars. No longer is it necessary to remove the front ones to reach the jars in the back. Another plus to the Sterilite drawers I purchased: they were the proper depths for refrigerator use.

THE FREEZER

You might also attack the kitchen freezer compartment. Mine was a disaster with all the little jars of this and that. By putting them in stacked drawers, I gained additional space. Properly packed, stacked food items will also suffer less freezer burn, a valuable added benefit.

If you plan to do much bulk food shopping and ingredient cooking, access to adequate freezer space is necessary. Some side-by-side kitchen refrigerator-freezers may provide ample space for your needs, but I couldn't survive without my garage upright – and I'm a single person. So buy one if you can.

A freezer doesn't have to be new. Check the newspaper ads and you're likely to find a good used one for well under $200. (The money you'll save by using it efficiently will pay for it.) An upright freezer in the garage or pantry is particularly handy for entertaining. It's great to have that shelf space for laying out individual dessert plates, decorative ice bowls, chilled glasses and extra ice.

Freezer Rules: This is a good place to mention some basic rules for freezing and making the best use of foods you freeze. Your freezer is a tremendous asset for preserving food, saving money and trips to the grocery, and allowing you to take advantage of fresh foods at their peak. Freezing is much easier and faster than canning, and more food values are retained. Large packages of meat, purchased at lower prices, can be cut, prepared and packaged the way you want them. So long as its contents are routinely rotated and used – not just hoarded – the freezer is an ideal food preservation tool.

Observe these rules:

Keep the freezer at or below zero temperature to avoid drawing moisture from food and contributing to its deterioration.

Chill food before freezing. Add unfrozen food a few pounds at a time to assure fast freezing and a stable temperature for other foods. Spread it out directly on the shelf or close to the sides in the coldest part of the freezer. When adding larger quantities, lower the freezer temperature and don't open the door for a couple of days; then the packages can be reorganized.

Keep the freezer nearly full to avoid cooling empty space. Freeze containers or zipper bags of water on empty shelves to fill the space and help keep the temperature at zero. Then, when you're heading for the boat, RV or campground, or transporting frozen food, you have ice blocks conveniently packed for the trip. When it melts you have drinking water.

Recommended Maximum Freezer Storage Times: These suggested storage limits apply assuming freezer temperatures are kept at or below zero, and that each item is carefully wrapped. You can, of course, store foods longer than the experts recommend – most of us do – but expect some deterioration in flavor, nutritional value, color and texture. As a target, try to use frozen items within six months. Foods that have been vacuum packed (shrink-wrapped) will, of course, maintain quality longer.

If your freezer gets opened too frequently (often the case with refrigerator freezing compartments), do not expect to maintain food quality even as long as the chart indicates.

Freezer burn is one obvious sign of deterioration, but should that occur, all is not lost. If, for example, a package of chicken breasts exhibits such signs, remove the damaged part and go on and cook the rest; it will be fine.

You must place commercially bagged frozen fruits and vegetables inside zippered freezer bags if they are to be kept for any length of time. Meats on styrofoam trays must always be completely repackaged with freezer-quality materials.

Bacon - 1 month
Beef, roasts, steaks - 8-12 months
Bread - 3-6 months
Butter, salted - 3 months
Butter, unsalted - 1 year
Clams, mussels in liquid - 3-6 months
Coffee, beans - 4-6 months
Coffee, ground - 1 month
Cooked meat - 2-3 months
Crab and shrimp - 6 months
Cream - 3-6 months
Fatty fish - 3 months
Fish frozen in water - 9 months

Frankfurters - 1-2 months
Fresh pasta - 2 months
Fruit, most -10 to 12 months
Ham - 2 months
Lean fish - 6 months
Meat loaf - 3 months
Meat, ground -3-4 months
Milk (whole) - 1 month
Nuts, shelled - 8 months
Onions (unblanched) - 3-6 months
Peppers (unblanched) - 3-6 months
Pork sausage 2-3 months
Pork, roasts, chops - 4-8 months
Poultry, cooked - 2-3 months
Poultry, uncooked - 9-12 months
Rice (cooked) 6 months
Scallops - 3 months
Stew meat - 2-3 months
Vegetables (blanched) - up to 1 year
Yeast, cakes - 6 months

FINDING THINGS IN THE FREEZER

If the freezer is to be your biggest ally for ingredient cooking, resign yourself to the fact that a modicum of organization is required. Try to keep like items together on shelves, in drawers or in boxes, so you can find them quickly.

Direct fish, fowl, meat and ice cream to the colder parts. (Be sure to keep part of the coldest area – usually the top shelf – accessible for fast-freezing items being added.) Prepared dishes go in one place, bakery items in another. Condiments, coffees, sauces, purees, nuts, juices, dairy products and small items can go in the door or in trays.

Incredibly organized people (I know three of the five living specimens) make up fancy computerized inventories and put them on the freezer door to keep track of what they have – some are even dated. Their inventory lists are protected inside plastic sheet holders. The quantities, however, are written in wax pencil on the outside like this: IIIIII. Say you have six pounds of butter and you remove one. Just rub off an "I," and you know what's left. In good conscience I cannot tell you I do this, but you've got to admit it is not a bad idea.

LABELING

Labeling is my least favorite organizing job. Certain that I will be able to identify what's in a freezer container three months from now, I try to get away with not doing it. So what if the pasta sauce turns out to be strawberries – have you never had strawberry pasta? Or the chili turns out to be gumbo? Doesn't everyone make mistakes?

This labeling chore is a fact of life, I guess, so visit the stationery store and get some nice-sized labels. All that needs to be on them are the contents, the date and any special instructions such as "add four cups of chicken broth," or "hold for Uncle Charlie – he'll eat anything."

—SHOPPING FOR STORAGE MATERIALS—

Here is a handy checklist of storage materials to help you review what's on hand and what you may need to buy from your warehouse or another supplier:

Aluminum foil
Canning jars
Food Saver Vacuum Seal System
Freezer wrap
Labels and marking pen
Plastic storage container set
Polyvinyl film
Rubberized shelf liner
Shelving units
Starbucks beverage bottles
Storage drawers
Upright freezer
Ziploc bags

—Foods To Keep On Hand—

IN THE FREEZER:
Bacon, raw, cooked bits
Bananas, pureed, muffins
Basil-pine nut pesto
Beans, cooked: black, kidney, navy, pinto
Beef, ground, sautéed with onions
Bell peppers: green, red, yellow,
    raw, roasted and/or pureed
Berries, whole and pureed
Bread cubes, croutons, crumbs
Brown sauce
Butter, garlic butter
Cakes
Carrots, cooked, raw
Celery, raw and cooked
Cheese, variety
Chicken, or turkey
Chicken broth, homemade
Chile peppers
Garlic, roasted and pureed
Garlic, fresh, sautéed in oil
Ginger
Gravy and roux
Ham hocks
Ham, diced, cooked
Ice cream, sherbet
Lemons, sliced, juice, grated rind
Lime juice, limeade (cans)
Louisiana hot links
Mangos, pureed
Milk, backup supply
Mushrooms, puree (duxelle)
Nuts: pecans, walnuts, almonds
Onions, raw and cooked
Oranges, sliced, juice, grated rind
Papayas, pureed
Peaches or nectarines, pureed, sliced in syrup
Pears, pureed
Pepperoni, sliced
Piecrusts, pies
Pork, cooked, shredded

Pork, sausage, browned
Salsas, various
Shrimp, raw and cooked
Spinach, blanched, whole or chopped
Tomatoes, cooked
White sauce

IN THE REFRIGERATOR:
Beverages
Butter
Cheese
Cottage cheese
Cream, milk, yogurt
Eggs
Fruits
Herbs
Horseradish
Jams, jellies, marmalades
Mayonnaise products
Sauces and seasonings, commercial
Vegetables

ON THE PANTRY SHELF:
Bread
Buttermilk powder
Canned goods
Chocolate, cocoa, baking
Flours, variety
Gelatin, plain
Herbs and spices
Honey
Oatmeal
Onions
Pasta, variety
Potatoes
Raisins
Rice, variety
Sugar: white, brown, powdered

That's it! This has to stop somewhere!

—INGREDIENT SUBSTITUTIONS—

Have you ever been in the mood for something chocolate, only to find you lacked the correct kind of chocolate? I can't count the times it has happened to me. Nowhere could I find instructions for substituting one for the other. Then, in the Summer 1984 issue of Southern Living, I found them. When using cocoa as a substitute for other chocolate in baking, be sure to decrease flour by the amount of cocoa added. Here is the cocoa "scoop."

1 (one ounce) square unsweetened chocolate =
3 tablespoons cocoa and 1 tablespoon shortening

1 (one ounce) envelope liquid baking chocolate =
3 tablespoons cocoa and 1 tablespoon of vegetable oil or melted shortening

1 (four ounce) bar sweet baking chocolate =
1/4 cup cocoa, 2 tablespoons plus 2 teaspoons shortening, and 1/4 cup plus 2 teaspoons sugar

1 (6-ounce) package semisweet chocolate morsels (1 cup) or 6 (one ounce) squares semisweet chocolate =
1/4 cup plus 2 tablespoons cocoa, 1/4 cup shortening, and 1/4 cup plus 3 tablespoons sugar

This is the most complete ingredient substitution list you'll find anywhere.

INGREDIENT	AMOUNT	SUBSTITUTE
ARROWROOT	1 tablespoon	2 1/4 t. cornstarch OR 1 1/2 T. all-purpose flour
BAKING POWDER	1 teaspoon	1/4 tsp. baking soda + 1/2 tsp. cream of tartar
BREAD CRUMBS	1 cup	3/4 c. soda crackers or 1 c. cornflake crumbs
BUTTER, for cooking and baking	1 cup	1 c. margarine; OR 7/8 c. vegetable oil, lard or shortening OR 4/5 c. bacon or chicken fat, strained
BUTTERMILK	1 cup	1 T. lemon juice or vinegar + milk to = 1 c. (it will thicken in minutes), OR 1 3/4 t. cream of tartar + 1 c. milk OR 1/4 c. buttermilk powder + 1 c. water
CATSUP	1 cup	1 c. tomato sauce + 1/2 c. sugar & 2 T. vinegar
CORN SYRUP, dark	1 cup	1 1/4 c. packed brown sugar + 1/4 c. water OR 3/4 c. light corn syrup + 1/4 c. water, OR 3/4 c. light corn syrup + 1/4 c. light molasses
CORN SYRUP, light	1 cup	1 1/4 c. granulated sugar + 1/4 c. water OR 1 c. maple syrup
CORNSTARCH	1 tablespoon	2 T. flour or 2 t. quick-cooking tapioca
CREAM, half and half, for cooking and baking	1 cup	1 1/2 T. melted butter in whole milk to = 1 c.
CREAM, heavy, for cooking and baking	1 cup	1/3 c. melted butter in 3/4 c. whole milk
CREAM, light, for cooking and baking	1 cup	3 T. melted butter in whole milk to = 1 c.
CREAM, sour, lowfat	3/4 cup	1/2 c. lowfat cottage cheese, 1/4 c. nonfat milk, 2 t. lemon juice processed in blender

INGREDIENT	AMOUNT	SUBSTITUTE
CREAM, sour, for and baking	1 cup	1 c. plain whole-milk yogurt OR 1 T. lemon juice in cooking evaporated whole milk to = 1 c. OR 1/4 c. buttermilk + 1/4 c. melted butter
FLOUR, cake	1 cup	1 c. all-purpose flour minus 2 T.
FLOUR, self-rising	1 cup	Add 1 1/2 t. baking power + 1/2 t. salt to all-purpose flour to = 1 level cup
FRUITFRESH POWDER, commercial,	1 quart of water	1 1/2 T. vinegar OR 3 T. lemon juice OR 1/2 c. white wine per quart of water
GARLIC, fresh	1 medium clove	1/8 t. powdered garlic OR 1/8 t. dried minced garlic
HERBS, fresh	1 T.	1 tsp. dried herbs
HONEY	1 cup	1 1/4 c. granulated sugar + 1/4 c. water or juice
MILK, whole	1 cup	1/2 c. evaporated milk + 1/2 c. water OR 4 T. powdered whole milk in 1 c. water OR 4 T. powdered skim milk + 2 T. butter in 1 c. water
MARSHMALLOWS, min.	10	1 large marshmallow
MUSTARD, dry	1 tsp.	1 T. prepared
SUGAR, dark brown	1 cup	4 T. molasses in 1 c. granulated sugar
SUGAR, light brown	1 cup	1/2 c. dark brown + 1/2 c. granulated sugar
SUGAR, superfine	1 cup	1 c. granulated whirled in blender
SUGAR, white	1 cup	1 3/4 c. confectioner's sugar
TOMATO JUICE	1 cup	1/2 c. tomato sauce + 1/2 c. water
TOMATO SAUCE	1 cup	1/2 c. tomato paste + 1/2 c. water
YEAST, dry	11/4oz pkg.	1 scant T. dry yeast OR 1 cake compressed

Here are some ingredients that can generally be used interchangeably, although in every case the results can't be guaranteed. The rule I follow is, if the substitution involves a small amount, it probably won't make much difference to the recipe's outcome. The larger the measure, the larger the risk.

IF RECIPE CALLS FOR	SUBSTITUTE
TOMATO SAUCE, sm. amount	Catsup
TOMATO PASTE, sm. amount	Tomato sauce
BUTTERMILK	Plain yogurt
CHEESE, cream	Cottage cheese, blended with milk
CHEESE, Parmesan	Romano cheese
CHEESE, ricotta	Cottage cheese, mashed, drained
MACE	Nutmeg
APPLES, chopped	Pears, with 1 T. lemon juice per cup
RAISINS	Currants
LEMON RIND, grated	Orange rind, grated
ITALIAN SAUSAGE	Pork sausage + fennel seed and oregano
LEEKS	Onions
COFFEE LIQUEUR IN CAKE	Strong brewed coffee
PUMPKIN IN PIE	Yams or sweet potatoes
CARROTS IN STEW	Turnips or parsnips
LIQUEURS	Flavored extracts
FLOUR TO THICKEN STEW OR SOUP	Cornstarch, arrowroot, egg yolks, bread crumbs, mashed potatoes, rice

PART IV:

Now, Let's Have

a

Dinner Party!

INTRODUCTION

Erase those words, "dinner party." Better to think of it as something more casual, more fun, less intimidating – maybe a chili party, a barbecue, or just plain supper. We don't need fear in our hearts at a time like this.

Before actually inviting people over for whatever you call it, consider for a moment the reasons people do not entertain more often. My own "official survey" brought forth these responses:

- The house is a mess
- Entertaining costs too much
- I don't have time to do it right
- Deciding on a menu is too difficult
- It might be a disaster

Let's take these objections one by one:

THE HOUSE IS A MESS.

My unwavering opinion on this subject emerged from a short period of fretting over "the condition of the house." It became clear that, if entertaining had to wait for a clean house, I would be old and gray before anyone crossed my doorway.

When my husband and I were both working and carrying a full college load in Kentucky, I was surrounded by world-class dustballs in our apartment that refused to go away, and regular attention to the problem was not an option. We could not afford evenings out in those days, so friendships were nurtured in our humble abode or at friends' homes. Early on I decided companionship took priority over dustballs, and I've never seriously regretted not being Mrs. Clean.

Your house does not have to be CLEAN. Presentable yes; clean, no. Your guests do not – I repeat – do not care if your house shows reasonable signs of human use. (Pigsty does not qualify as "reasonable.") They will be so pleased to be invited for a good time and a good meal that clean should not be an issue.

Learn to hide things, close some doors and get on with it. Life is too short. There is one room that should be ready for close scrutiny because that's where people will congregate – the kitchen. They'll be into the refrigerator, the oven, the kitchen drawers, and maybe even the pantry before you know it.

Whatever you do, have the house in what you consider a presentable state the day before the event. The only housework you will do on D-Day is clear off the kitchen counters, wave a feather duster around, and vacuum the living room if it obviously needs it.

ENTERTAINING COSTS TOO MUCH.

Warehouse shopping significantly reduces the cost of entertaining. When you have purchased food items in quantity and partially prepared them ahead, you will need less additional money for the last-minute shopping. Stock up on your favorite wines and liquors beforehand, when they are on sale. Buy inexpensive fresh flowers and do your own arrangements.

You don't need to serve lobster, caviar, expensive cuts of beef or truffles. Bean soup (see Caldo Gallego recipe) is a perfectly acceptable menu item on a cold fall evening. So are meatloaf and gravy, scalloped potatoes or macaroni and cheese. (Good old-fashioned, rib-sticking food is coming back into favor.)

A Coast Guard commander's wife in Juneau, Alaska, put together a fabulous array for a large party some years ago. Her ingenuity was the talk of the town. The dining room table was covered with oilcloth. The entire surface was a gorgeous flower consisting of lettuces, rows of sandwich meats, cheeses, pickles and olives, several kinds of bread, and bowls of mayonnaise and mustards. The guests had a great time preparing their own sandwiches. Then they made their own banana splits for dessert. She had a ball, and so did the guests.

As I get older and wiser, I've learned that simple menus are just fine – the important thing is that the hosts be relaxed and able to spend time with their guests.

I DON'T HAVE TIME TO DO IT RIGHT.

If you have spent any time at all with this book, you have learned the shopping strategies and secrets of ingredient cooking that enable you to easily combine fresh foods with the foods you have already prepared to various stages. The work is mostly done, which allows you to easily portray the image that puts guests at ease – that the event was no trouble at all, and you thoroughly enjoyed doing it.

What about cleanup? Woe be unto the host or hostess who insists on washing dishes and cleaning up while the party is in full swing. Noisy banging and clanging in the kitchen aside, the host belongs with the guests! The world will not come to an end if those dishes sit awhile. It's OK for a guest to help remove dishes from a course, and rinse and stack them, but that should take less than five minutes. Then, back to the table for the next course and conversation. There is always tomorrow, and procrastination is good in this case.

DECIDING ON THE MENU IS TOO DIFFICULT.

In case you'd like to use that excuse, included are some menus to get you off the hook and in the mood. I've used most of them as presented and know they go well together. (It's a good idea to keep a notebook of menus you serve, and to whom, so they don't get the same thing next time.)

IT MIGHT BE A DISASTER.

See "How to Avoid Last-minute Panic Attacks."

To summarize, my guiding principles for entertaining are to:

Do nearly all of the preparation in advance;
Have the kitchen clean and uncluttered;
Serve great-tasting food without spending a fortune;
Be relaxed to put guests at ease;
Recover from nervous breakdowns at least two hours before guests arrive.

— THE PRELIMINARIES: — PLANNING THE MENU

This discussion is for new cooks or people who haven't done much entertaining.
If you're experienced, skip this section altogether. However, even old pros might find something new in the section on
avoiding last-minute panic attacks. You may think these elements of menu planning are just good common sense, but it is
surprising the mistakes that can occur if you ignore them. Before deciding on the menu, you should run through each one:
Color, texture, taste, composition, temperature, smell, quantity and presentation. After doing this just once, it will come
automatically – sort of like hitting the right keys on a keyboard without looking.

COLOR

Haven't we all prepared a meal and suddenly noticed that it looked anemic? Why did we do that? Would you want a light-colored seafood appetizer, fettucine Alfredo, cornbread, a yellow molded salad, crookneck squash and lemon pie served on white plates over a white tablecloth?

___Yes ___No   (Answer: No)

Some foods are dull in color; they should be contrasted with bright, primary colored foods. Try to include something red, yellow, green, white, orange, or mixtures of several colors. You don't want to serve green peas, spinach and a green salad at the same meal.

Achieving a good variety of colors in your menu is easy to do. If you notice too much of one color, add a bit of contrasting color; for instance, red bell pepper, black olives, parsley or minced green onions to offset the white rice, grits, potatoes or pasta.

Take a moment to picture all the items that will go on the dinner plate. How do they look together?

TEXTURE

Just as important as color to a meal's attractiveness is having a variety of textures. Think airy, dense, chewy, soft, crunchy, velvety, flaky, firm, dry, wet, and use your imagination to achieve a reasonable variety. Mix raw with cooked foods. Picture the entire menu from this perspective.

TASTE

The third thing to consider is offering a friendly combination of tastes. I've seen more than one dinner party meet the other criteria and fail by mixing the wrong foods. Too many spicy dishes, too many containing cheese, the same predominant seasoning used in several dishes – you get the idea. You also need to be careful mixing ethnic foods to be sure they complement each other. Eclectic is good, but don't pair the Mexican dish with the shrimp curry.

197

COMPOSITION

With many of us health and weight-conscious, the considerate host offers a low-calorie, low-fat appetizer with the buttery stuffed mushrooms or fat-laden cheeses. Serve a fruit salsa next to the guacamole. Regular and low-fat tortilla chips. For the main course, limit the sinful dishes to one or two, forgoing your favorite cheesecake if the main course breaks the fat/calorie barrier. There's nothing wrong with serving a refreshing sorbet after a rich meal. Balance the dessert with the meal.

Because most people are willing to splurge a little when invited over for dinner, I tend to take liberties with the menu that I don't do on a regular basis. If my recipes call for butter, guests will get butter. However, with a little experimentation, you'll find margarine, fat-free mayonnaise, light cream, or sugar, egg, and sour cream substitutes, etc., work just fine in any number of them.

TEMPERATURE

More variety called for. It's good to have an icy, cold dish, another served at room temperature, one or more hot ones and perhaps even a frozen one. Again, think balance. Follow hot appetizers with a chilled salad. Hot food should be served hot. A mistake I have often made was assuming that, because the serving dish was hot, the ingredients were, too. Test it first.

Especially when serving pasta, heated plates are a must. (You can store them in the dishwasher, turning on the dry cycle before the meal.)

SMELL

A few foods just don't smell good when they're cooking. Avoid them, or precook them and reheat in the microwave. Plan something that smells divine when your guests come in the door – bread rising in the machine is a winner, a pork roast, a fruit pie finishing up in the oven. If the menu doesn't qualify, bring out the potpourri. A small teapot with simmering citrus peels or vanilla, cinnamon, cloves and bay leaves will do the trick.

Party Hint:

> *Keep beer and soft drinks cold in the dishwasher.*
> *Put plenty of ice in the bottom, then arrange drinks on the ice. Put more ice on top.*
> *Melted ice goes down the drain.*

QUANTITY

More is not better. Think of the parties you've attended where there was way too much food, and too many different kinds of food. And the hosts looked offended because half of it was uneaten. Who hasn't "maxed-out" only to be presented with a heavy dessert that you feel obligated to down since the cook "went to all that trouble"?

Go light on the appetizers if the dinner is substantial or vice versa. The idea is to serve a well-balanced, healthful, delicious, meal of modest proportions, so your guests don't feel gorged, wishing they had a stomach pump.

PRESENTATION

The simplest food can be special if arranged in attractive serving dishes. No old cooking pots, skillets or ugly bakeware allowed. Be on the lookout for great serving dishes; they don't have to match. In fact, it's better if they don't.

Rosie Porter, a well-known Alaska publisher who has since defected to California, set the most unusual table I've seen. Aside from being able to accommodate more than 20 at her Bethel table, she provided each guest with his or her own unique fine china place setting from her collection. Imagine, no two china patterns alike! How wonderfully original, and beautiful.

— INVITING THE GUESTS —

FORMAL DINNER PARTIES:

Invitations. Just about anything goes for handling invitations these days. Even Miss Manners approves of invitations being sent via fax or email. They can be just as decorative and appropriate, thanks to computer art, as printed invitations sent by "snailmail," and just as welcome. A telephoned invitation usually gets an immediate RSVP, which is necessary when you're inviting on short notice. Of course, the earlier you issue the invitation – within reason – the more likely you are to get a positive response.

Allergies and Special Diets. When someone new to your circle responds by phone, be sure to ask if he or she has any food allergies. A friend of mine becomes immediately ill if she swallows even part of a macadamia nut! (Attending to a stricken guest while waiting for the medics can be disruptive.) Some people are vegetarians or are on special diets, and they are generally thoughtful enough to let you know without even asking. While you can usually accommodate these needs during the menu-planning, it's perfectly acceptable for a guest to bring along an entrée.

The Guest List. In my house, sit-down dinners are limited by my dining room table to eight people, or ten with a leaf added. Six to eight people are most often invited, and lively conversation is seldom lacking. I never worry about having all couples or the same number of men as women for one of these – people are invited for themselves. I do let everyone know it is a sit-down dinner and what time the food will be served.

BUFFET DINNERS:

Guest counts for buffets typically number 15 to 20 except for family events, which can involve around 30. Fortunately, these are nearly always potluck, or there would be definite logistics problems in my current kitchen. People can come and go more casually with the buffet format, and this allows some guests to attend who might not otherwise be able to comply with a strict serving schedule.

I've done cocktail parties with heavy hors d'oeuvres for 150 at home, but I don't recommend this as a weekly – or even monthly – activity. There is a rule for buffets I've learned from experience (hauling leftover food to a shelter) and that is: "The more people you have, the less food you need."

Seating for buffets is "anywhere there's a vacant spot." You don't need tray tables, but their absence means serving only food that doesn't require a knife. Both Emily Post and Miss Manners demand an appropriate eating surface but, in many of our homes, that simply is not possible. Besides, some rules are meant to be broken.

A riotously successful party I had once involved all the guests sprawled out on a sheet of Visqueen that covered the entire living room, eating fresh King Crab and a hearty salad, and tossing the shells (yes, at each other) with abandon. (Talk about an easy cleanup: We picked up the four corners of the "tablecloth" and threw the entire mess in the garbage.)

Cancellations. The bane of a host is the last-minute cancellation. Except in cases of extreme emergency (the guest's death would qualify), cancellations can be more than irritating. The fewer the guests, the greater the offense. There is no acceptable way, unfortunately, to let the person know you consider him or her an ungracious dolt for such behavior.

Even worse is the person who just doesn't show, and you keep waiting. In this case, withholding future invitations for at least twenty years is a reasonable sentence. You would, of course, relent upon receiving a heart-wrenching note of apology and a bouquet of your favorite expensive flowers.

HOW TO AVOID LAST-MINUTE PANIC ATTACKS

If you read the last section, you've already considered most of the contingencies, but something will go wrong – count on it. You burned the rolls. The roast is in the oven and the power is out. A kitchen fire. Two "maybes" you thought wouldn't come, did, and you're short two chairs. The phone keeps ringing, and the sink is stopped up.

There are only two things to do: (a) Laugh it off, or (b) Don't mention it, and go to Plan C. A good sense of humor is imperative here. Sure, you want everything perfect, but the guests don't care – they're just happy to enjoy the good company and a meal they didn't have to cook. The moral is: "Don't sweat the small stuff."

Naturally, organized "you" will have set the table the day before, but last-minute details, answering the door, and people underfoot can still cause you to be frazzled. Eliminate potential interruptions after guests arrive by "walking through" the dinner, step by step, before their arrival. Here are some matters you'll want resolved before the guests arrive.

Even if you're not the King or Queen of Lists, you need some basic organizational tools. A list is basic. Use this one or make up your own.

The List.

Is there room on the table for serving dishes? How will they be placed?

Are serving utensils placed next to the serving dishes?

Are stove burners or ovens available for last-minute heating?

Will the serving dish fit in the microwave, and is it heatsafe?

Does an oven dish require the same temperature as the dinner rolls?

Are trivets for hot dishes on the table?

Is a corkscrew handy? Wine at the right temperatures?

Did you bag or buy extra ice? Is the ice bucket filled?

Are wine or cocktail glasses arranged with the beverages?

Are non-alcoholic beverages set out?

Has background music been selected? Lighting set?

Have plates been chilled or heated?

Will guests sit anywhere or are seats assigned?

Are there coat hangers and enough room in the guest closet?

Is the doberman restrained?

SPECIAL TOUCHES

Whatever you do to add a special flair to formal dinner parties will add to their charm. Clever place cards. Miniature flower arrangements at each place setting. Fresh flowers or mint in straws to decorate beverage glasses. Cherries, mint or pieces of fruit frozen in ice cubes. Heated or chilled dishes and utensils. Bread baked and served in a flower pot. A centerpiece made of carved vegetables.

Decorated Ice Bowl. Two years ago when my begonias, geraniums, snapdragons and pansies were in full bloom, I ventured into creating ice bowls in which fresh flowers were frozen. I made several for my brother Rick's wedding reception. It took a few tries before mastering the technique, but it really is pretty simple; plus, you can use them more than once if they don't thaw. Here's how:

Cover the bottom of a large metal or plastic mixing bowl with 11/2 inches of boiling water.

Freeze solid. Set a smaller bowl on top of the ice layer and pour a small amount of boiling water around to level and anchor it. Weight it down. Freeze. Slide a row of blossoms (facing outward) or greenery down around the outside of the smaller bowl. Cover the bottom of the blossoms with hot water, again just to anchor them, and freeze. Add more water and freeze that, then another row of flowers.

Keep it up until you've made the ice bowl as deep as you want. When finished, remove both bowls (with warm water or hair dryer to barely loosen them), leaving just the decorated ice. On the serving table, set the ice bowl on a larger dish to catch the water as the ice melts. Put greenery around the bowl if desired. You can even line it with plastic film to assure the ice won't melt into the salad. These creations can be truly stunning.

Party Hint:

> *Heat dinner plates, soup bowls or serving dishes in the dishwasher.*
> *Before serving, run them through the "dry" cycle.*

201

DINNER PARTY MENUS

The recipes in these menus have been served at one time or another to appreciative guests.
They were selected to help make entertaining easy; very little last-minute preparation is involved.
You don't need to serve as many items as are listed in each menu, especially not for informal get-togethers.
You could, from the first menu, serve just the chili and cornbread for the main course, and the custard for dessert.
When you want to "put on the dog," however, use the complete menus.

Strawberry-Watermelon Margaritas
•
Chile Shrimp Divine
•
World's Best Gazpacho
•
Chili with Pork and Pintos
•
Mexican Cornbread
•
Steamed Orange Custard

Gorgeous Guacamole, Peach Salsa
•
Roasted Orange and Yellow Pepper Soup
•
Dishwasher Fish
•
Grilled Asparagus
•
Cherry Cobbler with Amaretto Cream

Asparagus-stuffed Prosciutto
•
Orange, Onion and Cilantro Salad
•
Glenda's Cioppino
•
Garlic Bread
•
Double Musky Carrot Cake

Kris's Killer Peach Gin Freeze
•
Cindy's Oriental Walnuts
•
Fresh Tomato Soup with Garlic Croutons
•
Hawaiian Coleslaw
•
Beef Noodle Casserole
•
Mango Velvet

Stuffed Artichokes with Mushrooms
•
Roasted Green Pepper and Tomato Salad
•
Caldo Gallego with Peasant Bread
•
Homemade Applesauce
•
Vanilla Ice Cream with Chocolate Hazelnut
Sauce

Spiced Nuts, Baked Brie
•
Roast Prime Rib with Yorkshire Pudding
•
Garlic Spinach
•
Beaumont Inn Corn Pudding
•
Oriental Coleslaw
•
Peaches in Wine

Cheese Tray
•
Japanese Marinated Cucumbers
•
Kathryn's Spicy Thai Chicken Pasta
•
Lemon Ice in Lemon Cups

Stuffed Strawberries, Mango Salsa
•
Diane's Lemon-Pepper Pasta with Shrimp
•
Mixed Salad Greens with Pine Nut Dressing
•
Sweet Potato Spice Cake

Orange Avocado Cilantro Soup
in Cantaloupe Shells
•
Paella Valenciana
•
Crusty Roasted Garlic Bread
•
Strawberries with Sour Cream and Brown Sugar

Cream of Broccoli Soup
•
Shredded Chicken-filled Tortillas
•
Black Bean and Pepper Salad
•
Baked Stuffed Onions #1
•
Baked Bananas with Brandied Raisins

Simple Stuffed Mushrooms
•
Grilled Italian Sausages
•
Broccoli with Wine Sauce
•
Roasted Garlic Mashed Potatoes
•
Mixed Fruit Salad with Citrus Dressing
•
Ice Cream with Lemon-Ginger Syrup

Potato Onion Tortilla with
Homemade Chili Sauce
•
Carrot, Raisin and Pineapple Salad
•
Mexican Chili Pie
•
Cheesecake with Strawberry Sauce

Stuffed Cucumbers
•
Red Pepper Soup with Garlic Croutons
•
Roast Chicken with Mariano's Poultry Stuffing
•
Asparagus with Cheese Sauce
•
Mashed Potatoes and Gravy
•
Apple Pie with Vanilla Ice Cream

Lemon Pecans, Cambozola Cheese with
Water Crackers
•
Caesar Salad
•
Okra, Corn and Tomatoes, Southern Style
•
Gail's Rum-baked Salmon
•
Peach Cobbler

Greek Lemon Soup
•
Sun-dried Tomatoes, Cheese and Mushroom
Pizza
•
Shrimp and Pine Nut Salad
•
Orange Sherbet with Peach Schnapps

Walnut Stuffed Mushrooms
•
Grapefruit and Avocado Salad
•
Pork Medallions
•
Pan-seared Vegetables
•
Blueberry Frozen Yogurt

203

Pineapple Salsa
•
Pork Ribs with Spicy Barbecue Sauce
•
Mom's Cottage Cheese Salad
•
Sweet and Sour Spinach Salad
•
Old-fashioned Bread Pudding with Lemon Sauce

Kathryn's Black Bean Dip with Salsa
•
Cream of Asparagus Soup
•
Kelly's Lemon-pepper Halibut
•
Louisiana Candied Yams
•
Spinach Salad with Simon & Seafort's
Egg-mustard Dressing
•
Granny's Black Walnut Applesauce Cake

Pineapple Daquiris
•
Caponata with Toasted French Bread
•
Fefi's Cuban Black Beans and Rice
•
Spinach, Scallop and Mushroom Salad
•
Blazing Bananas

Ceviche
•
Linguini with Basil Pine Nut Pesto
•
Garlic Spinach
•
Pineapple Walnut Upside-down Cake

Banana Slush
•
Baked Potatoes
•
Broccoli Salad
•
Dishwasher Fish
•
Poached Pears, Cherries and Prunes

Maritata Soup
•
Wanda LaFleur's Dirty Rice
•
Crab-stuffed Avocado
•
Peach Pineapple Yogurt Ice Cream

—INDEX—

This index is designed to be a useful reference for warehouse food shoppers. It answers the question: "How can I use the rest of this (fruit, vegetable, chicken, meat, etc.)? While most cookbooks index recipes only by their primary ingredients, this one does much more. If the recipe contains as little as one cup of a particular food, the recipe is listed under that food category. For instance, Paella Valenciana is listed under "Rice," "Onions," "Peppers," "Seafood," and "Tomatoes."

Checking the index to get ideas for other ways to use your food supplies will save considerable time and money. No more searching through your cookbooks to find out what to do with extra chicken broth, lemons, mushrooms or what have you. The information is right here!

APPENDIX

LOCATIONS OF SAM'S CLUB
WAREHOUSES AS OF JANUARY 1999

ALABAMA
Dothan
Florence
Homewood
Huntsville
Irondale
Mobile
Montgomery
Tuscaloosa

ALASKA
Anchorage (2)
Fairbanks

ARIZONA
Flagstaff
Gilbert-Phoenix SE
Phoenix (3)
Tucson
Yuma

ARKANSAS
Ft. Smith
Little Rock (2)
Springdale

CALIFORNIA
Cathedral City
Chino
City of Industry
Concord
Downey
El Monte
Fountain Valley
Fullerton
Gardena
Irvine
Montclair
Oxnard
Rancho Cordova
Riverside
Roseville
Sacramento (2)
San Bernardino
San Fernando
Southgate
Stanton
Torrance
Vacaville
Yuba City

COLORADO
Arvada
Aurora

Colorado Springs (2)
Denver
Ft. Collins
Grand Junction
Littleton (2)
Loveland
Pueblo

CONNECTICUT
Berlin
Manchester
Orange

DELAWARE
Dover

FLORIDA
Brandon
Clearwater
Coral Springs
Daytona Beach
Ft. Myers
Ft. Pierce
Ft. Walton Beach
Gainesville
Jacksonville (3)
Lakeland
Lantana
Melbourne
Miami
Miramar
Naples
New Port Richey
Ocala
Orlando (4)
Panama City Beach
Pensacola
Pinellas Park (2)
Port Charlotte
Sarasota
Sunrise
Tallahassee
Tampa (2)
Vero Beach
W. Palm Beach

GEORGIA
Albany
Atlanta
Atlanta-West
Augusta
Bogart
Buckhead
Columbus

Duluth
Gainesville
Macon
Marietta
Rome
Roswell
Savannah
Tucker
Valdosta

HAWAII
Pearl City

IDAHO
Idaho Falls

ILLINOIS
Addison
Champaign
Cicero
Crystal Lake
Decatur
Des Plaines
Evanston
Evergreen Park
Gurnee
Hodgkins
Joliet
Lansing
Marion
Matteson
Naperville
Northlake
O'Fallon
Peoria
Rockford
Springfield
Streamwood
Tinley Park
Wheeling
Woodridge

INDIANA
Bloomington
Davenport
Evansville
Fishers
Ft. Wayne
Goshen
Greenwood
Indianapolis (3)
Kokomo
Lafayette

Merrillville
Mishawaka
Terre Haute

IOWA
Ames
Cedar Rapids
Council Bluffs
Davenport
Des Moines
Sioux City
Waterloo

KANSAS
Kansas City
Salina
Topeka
Wichita (2)

KENTUCKY
Florence
Lexington
Louisville (2)
Paducah

LOUISIANA
Alexandria
Baton Rouge
Gretna
Lafayette
Lake Charles
Monroe
New Orleans (2)
Shreveport

MAINE
Augusta
Bangor
Scarborough

MARYLAND
Annapolis
Baltimore (2)
Frederick
Gaithersburg
Hagerstown
Hyattsville
Laurel
Salisbury
Waldorf

MASSACHUSETTS
Natick
Seekonk

Worcester

MICHIGAN
Battle Creek
Comstock Park
Farmington Hills
Flint
Holland
Jackson
Kentwood
Lansing
Madison Heights
Muskegon
Port Huron
Portage
Roseville
Saginaw
Southfield
Southgate
Traverse City
Utica
Waterford
Westland
Ypsilanti

MINNESOTA
Burnsville
Fridley
Hermantown
Inver Grove Hts.
Mankato
Rochester
St. Cloud
St. Louis Park
White Bear Lake

MISSISSIPPI
Gulfport
Hattiesburg
Jackson
Tupelo

MISSOURI
Cape Girardeau
Columbia
Ferguson
Joplin
Kansas City (3)
Springfield
St. Louis (4)

MONTANA
Great Falls

NEBRASKA
Grand Island
Lincoln
Omaha

NEW YORK
Albany
Big Flats
Cheektowaga
Clay
Colonie
Ellicott
Elmsford
Fishkill
Greece
Henrietta
Kingston
Medford
Middletown
Niagara Falls
Plattsburgh
Syracuse
Vestal
Watertown

NEW HAMPSHIRE
Concord
Hudson
Manchester
Seabrook
NEVADA
Las Vegas (2)

NEW JERSEY
Delran Township
Deptford
East Brunswick
Freehold
Pleasantville
Princeton

NEW MEXICO
Albuquerque
Farmington
Santa Fe

NORTH CAROLINA
Asheville
Cary
Charlotte (3)
Fayetteville
Gastonia
Goldsboro
Greensboro
Hickory
Jacksonville
Raleigh (2)
Wilmington
Winston-Salem
Winterville

NORTH DAKOTA
Fargo
Grand Forks

OHIO
Beavercreek
Boardman
Brooklyn
Cincinnati (4)
Columbus (2)
Dayton
Dayton
Elyria
Fairlawn
Lima
Niles
North Canton
Oakwood Village
Ontario
Reynoldsburg
South Point
St. Clairsville
Toledo
Willoughby Hills

OKLAHOMA
Lawton
Oklahoma City (3)
Tulsa (2)

PENNSYLVANIA
Altoona
Dothan
Easton
Erie
Harrisburg
Hatboro
Langhorne
Monroeville
Muncy
Philadelphia
Pittsburgh (2)
Reading
Scranton
State College
West Mifflin
Whitehall
Wilkes-Barre
York

RHODE ISLAND
Warwick

SOUTH CAROLINA
Anderson
Columbi a (2)
Florence
Greenville
Hilton Head
Myrtle Beach
N. Charleston
Spartanburg

SOUTH DAKOTA
Rapid City
Sioux Falls

TENNESSEE
Chattanooga
Clarksville
Jackson
Kingsport
Knoxville (2)
Memphis (2)
Murfreesboro
Nashville (3)

TEXAS
Abilene
Addison
Amarillo
Austin (2)
Beaumont
Brownsville
College Station
Conroe
Corpus Christi
Dallas (5)
El Paso (3)
Fort Worth
Grand Prairie
Houston (8)
Humble
Laredo
Lewisville
Longview
Lubbock
Lufkin
Mc Allen
Midland
Odessa
Plano
Richland Hills
San Antonio (4)
San Luis Potosi
Sherman
Temple
Texarkana
Texas City
Tyler
Victoria
Waco
White Settlement
Wichita Falls

UTAH
Layton
Murray
Ogden
Provo
Salt Lake City

VIRGINIA
Bluefield
Charlottesville
Chesapeake
Colonial Heights
Lynchburg
Midlothian
Newport News
Richmond
Roanoke
Woodbridge

WASHINGTON
Fife
Seattle

WEST VIRGINIA
Fairmont
South Charleston
Vienna

WISCONSIN
Appleton
Eau Claire
Franklin
Green Bay
Madison
Milwaukee
Onalaska
Racine
Waukesha
Wausau
West Allis

WYOMING
Casper
Cheyenne

Worldwide Web Address: http:\\ www.samsclub.com

LOCATIONS OF COSTCO WAREHOUSES AS OF JANUARY 1999

U.S.A.

ALASKA
Anchorage
N. Anchorage
Juneau

ARIZONA
Glendale
Mesa
Phoenix
Prescott
Scottsdale
Superstition Springs
Tempe
Thomas Road
Tucson
NW Tucson

CALIFORNIA
Alhambra
Antioch
Azusa
Bakersfield
Burbank
Cal Expo
Canoga Park
Carlsbad
Carmel Mountain
Chico
Chino Hills
Chula Vista
City of Industry
Clovis
Coachella Valley
Corona
Danville
El Centro
Eureka
Fairfield
Foster City
Fountain Valley
Fremont
Fresno
Fullerton
Garden Grove
Goleta (2)
Hawthorne
Hayward
  (Bus. Center)
Inglewood
Irvine
La Mesa
Laguna Niguel
Lancaster
Livermore
Los Feliz
Martinez
Merced
Modesto
Montebello
Moreno Valley
Mountain View
Northridge
Norwalk
Novato
Oxnard
Rancho Cordova
Rancho Cucamonga
Rancho del Rey
Redding
Redwood City
Richmond
Roseville
Sacramento
Salinas
San Bernardino
San Bruno
San Diego
SE San Diego
San Francisco
S. San Francisco
San Jose (2)
San Juan Capistrano
San Leandro
San Marcos
Sand City
Santa Clara
Santa Clarita
Santa Cruz
Santa Maria
Santa Rosa
Santee
Signal Hill
Simi Valley
Stockton
Sunnyvale
Torrance
Temecula
Tustin
Vallejo
Van Nuys
Victorville
Visalia
Vista
Westlake Village
Yorba Linda

COLORADO
Aurora
Denver
SW Denver
Westminster

DELAWARE
Christiana

CONNECTICUT
Brookfield
Milford
Waterbury

FLORIDA
Altamonte Springs
Davie
Delray Beach
Kendall
Lantana
Miami
Miami Lakes
N. Miami Beach
Palm Beach Gardens
Pompano Beach
S. Orlando

GEORGIA
Gwinnett
Perimeter
Town Center

HAWAII
Hawaii Kai
Honolulu
Kailua-Kona
Maui

IDAHO
Boise
Twin Falls

ILLINOIS
Oak Brook
Schaumburg
Chicago (2)

MARYLAND
Beltsville
Gaithersburg
Glen Burnie
White Marsh

MASSACHUSETTS
Avon
Danvers
Dedham
W. Springfield
Waltham

MICHIGAN
Bloomfield
Livonia I
Livonia II
Madison Heights
Roseville

DELAWARE
Christiana

MONTANA
Billings
Bozeman
Kalispell
Missoula

NEVADA
Henderson
Las Vegas
Reno

NEW HAMPSHIRE
Nashua

NEW JERSEY
Brick Township
Clifton
Edison
E. Hanover
Hackensack
Hazlet
Union
Wayne
Wharton

NEW MEXICO
Albuquerque

NEW YORK
Brooklyn
Commack
Holbrook
Lawrence
Melville
Nanuet
Nesconset
New Rochelle
Queens
Staten Island
Westbury

OREGON
Aloha
Bend
Clackamas
Eugene
Medford
Portland
Salem
Tigard
Warrenton

PENNSYLVANIA
King of Prussia
Lancaster

UTAH
Midvale
Salt Lake City

VERMONT
Colchester

VIRGINIA
Chesterfield
Fairfax
Hampton
Harrisonburg
Manassas
Newington
Norfolk
Pentagon City
Sterling
W. Henrico
Winchester

WASHINGTON
Aurora Village
Bellingham
Clarkston
Everett
E. Wenatchee
Federal Way
Issaquah
Kennewick
Kirkland
Lynnwood
  (Bus. Center)
Seattle
Sequim
Silverdale
Spokane
N. Spokane
Tacoma
Tukwila
Tumwater
Union Gap
Union

219

ALBERTA
N. Calgary
S. Calgary
Edmonton
N. Edmonton
S. Edmonton
Grande Prairie
Lethbridge
Red Deer

BRITISH COLUMBIA
Abbotsford
Burnaby
Kamloops
Kelowna
Nanaimo
Port Coquitlam
Prince George
Richmond
Surrey
Vancouver

MANITOBA
E. Winnipeg
Winnipeg

NEWFOUNDLAND
St. John's

NEW BRUNSWICK
Moncton

NOVA SCOTIA
Halifax

ONTARIO
Ajax
Ancaster
Barrie
Brampton
Burlington
Etobicoke
Gloucester
Kingston
Kitchener
London
Markham
Mississauga
Mississauga N.
Nepean
St. Catharines
Scarborough

Vaughan
Windsor

QUÉBEC
Anjou
Brossard
Chicoutimi
Gatineau
Laval
Marché Central
Montréal
Pointe Claire
Québec
Sainte-Foy
Saint-Hubert
Saint-Jérôme
Sherbrooke
Trois-Rivières-Ouest

SASKATCHEWAN
Regina
Saskatoon

AGUASCALIENTES
Aguascalientes

BAJA
Mexicali
Tijuana

GUANAJUATO
León

GUERRERO
Acapulco

MEXICO, D.F.
Coapa
Mixcoac
Satélite

MICHOACAN
Morelia

JALISCO
Guadalajara
Monterrey

QUERÉTARO
Querétaro

SONORA
Hermosillo

YUCATÁN
Mérida

You can visit Costco on the World Wide Web at http://www.costco.com

ORDER FORM

By telephone:
Merril Press, Bellevue, Washington,
1-425-454-7009

By fax:
1-425-451-3959

By mail:
Merril Press, Box 1682, Bellevue, Washington 98009

On line:
http:/www.amazon.com or www.merrilpress.com

Please send _____ copies of Paula Easley's WAREHOUSE FOOD COOKBOOK
at $22.95 each to:

Name_____

Address _____

City, State, Zip _____

Telephone _____

Sales Tax:
For California orders add 7.75% sales tax

Shipping:
Add $4.50 per book

Payment Method:
__ Check
__ Credit Card: __ VISA __ MasterCard

Card Number: _____ Exp. Date_____

READER IDEA SUBMISSION CARD

My suggestions to improve future editions of the Warehouse Food Cookbook:

_____

_____

What I liked most about this book:

_____

_____

Tips for helping cooks manage bulk food purchases:

_____

_____

Ways I save money while buying big:

_____

_____

Entertaining secrets I'd like to share with readers:

_____

_____

Include this recipe in a future edition:

_____

_____

Return this card or additional pages to:
Merril Press, Box 1682, Bellevue, Washington 98009.
Or, email the author at paula.easley@usa.net.

PERMISSION: If my ideas are included in future editions, please credit my name, city and state as follows:

_____

_____